W9-AYN-867

Collection Development and Resources Access Plan for the Skokie Public Library

Collection Development and Resources Access Plan for the Skokie Public Library

Written by Teri Room, Coordinator of Collection Development,
and the Librarians of the Skokie Public Library
Revision coordinated by Barbara A. Kozlowski, Associate Director for Public Services

Skokie Public Library Trustees
Diana Hunter, President/President Emerita
John Graham, Vice President
Dayle Zelenka, Secretary
Richard Basofin/Susan Greer
Zelda Rich/John M. Wozniak

Director
Carolyn A. Anthony

5215 Oakton Street
Skokie, Illinois 60077
http://www.skokie.lib.il.us

2008
3rd Edition
1998
2nd Edition
1990
1st Edition

ISBN-10: 0-8389-8506-8
ISBN-13: 978-0-8389-8506-9
2008

Collection Development and Resources Access Plan for the Skokie (Illinois) Public Library
Distributed by the Public Library Association, a division of the American Library Association.
www.pla.org

CONTENTS

I. PURPOSE

The purpose of the *Collection Development and Resources Access Plan* is twofold. It is a comprehensive document to guide both present and future selectors in the process of developing the collection to meet the needs of Skokie's ever-changing community. The statement also provides a clear outline of the roles, duties, and responsibilities of all persons involved in the selection of materials. Further, it sets out a consistent plan for the management and development of the collection, thus giving direction to the allocation of the materials budget.

The second purpose of the *Collection Development and Resources Access Plan* is to explain to new staff, to professionals in other libraries, and to the community the history, mission, and objectives of the library's collection so they can better understand the rationale behind the selection of materials and resources. In this area, the statement affirms the principles upon which selection is based and the policies and goals for managing the collection. The descriptions of each area of the collection should help people develop realistic expectations about the scope and depth of the library's holdings.

II. RESOURCES SELECTION

A. Community Description

The Village of Skokie is a multiethnic community of about 69,000 located just 13 miles north of Chicago's downtown area known as the Loop. A strong retail base provides substantial tax revenue, allowing property taxes to remain relatively low while village services are maintained at a high level. Skokie ranks 6th in the state of Illinois in wholesale trade, 13th in the state in retail sales, 7th in the number of manufacturing businesses, and 12th in manufacturing employment. Transportation to Chicago is convenient via the Edens Expressway, the Chicago Transit Authority's (CTA) Skokie Swift rail line, and Pace and CTA bus routes. Skokie's total labor force is 37,349.

Housing is primarily single-family homes (14,823) with a median value of $396,300 in 2006. Seventy-five percent of housing units are owner occupied. The population of Skokie is predominantly white, with 23% Asian and 6% African American residents. The community is multiethnic, with 7.3% Hispanic and 8.8% Asian Indian residents. There are also significant populations of Russian, Chinese, Filipino, and Korean residents. The median age is listed as 40.6, and average household size is 3.04. Youth aged 0–18 is estimated at 25% of the population while those 65 and over comprise 13% of the residents. The median age has been decreasing in recent years, and schools have recorded an increasing enrollment as homes once occupied by long-time residents are purchased by younger families. The biggest growth in recent years has been in the population of teens, 20–24 year olds, and the over–85 population.

Within the village are six public elementary school districts, two high school districts (Niles Township with two schools and Evanston Township with one), nine parochial schools (five Jewish, three Catholic, and one Lutheran), National-Louis University, and the Ray Hartstein Campus of Oakton Community College. Other educational institutions include Maine Oakton Niles Northfield Adult Continuing Education Program (MONNACEP) for adult noncredit education, the Hebrew Theological Seminary, and the Orchard Village for mildly mentally handicapped young adults. The Skokie Park District, Mayer Kaplan Jewish Children's Center, Albert J. Smith Activities Center for Seniors, and the 16 churches and 10 synagogues offer recreational and educational programs to the community. Skokie is also a short drive from important educational institutions such as Northwestern University, DePaul University, Loyola University, and more. Almost all of these institutions offer nondegree programs and classes in addition to numerous degree-granting programs. It is not surprising that 89% of the residents of Skokie over the age of 25 have completed at least 12 years of school and 40.4% have a bachelor's degree or higher.

Important cultural organizations in the community include the Skokie Fine Arts Commission; the North Shore Center for the Performing Arts, home to Northlight Theatre, the Skokie Valley Symphony, and Centre East; Skokie Northshore Sculpture Park; Skokie Theatre Music Foundation; the Skokie Historical Society; the Skokie Heritage Museum; and the Illinois Holocaust Museum and Education Center. Skokie has been home to the largest number of Holocaust survivors in the United States. Skokie is also a short drive from Chicago and its leading cultural institutions such as the Art Institute, Lyric Opera,

Skokie—Population by Age Group

Age Group	1990 Census		2000 Census		2006 American Community Survey Group	
	Number	Percent	Number	Percent	Number	Percent
0–4	3,029	5.1%	3,265	5.2%	4,201	5.7%
5–14	6,815	11.5%	8,322	13.2%	10,123	13.7%
15–19	3,385	5.7%	4,400	6.9%	6,307	8.5%
20–24	2,935	4.9%	3,010	4.8%	5,388	7.3%
25–34	7,729	13.0%	6,489	10.2%	6,351	8.6%
35–54	15,866	26.7%	19,135	30.2%	22,569	30.5%
55–64	7,347	12.4%	6,341	10%	9,249	12.5%
65–85+	12,326	20.7%	12,386	19.5%	9,733	13.2%
TOTAL	59,432	100.0%	63,348	100.0%	73,921	100.0%

Chicago Symphony, Field Museum of Natural History, Steppenwolf Theatre, Goodman Theater, and more. Many Skokie residents are active members of these institutions and attend their programs.

Employment of residents is diversified, with 23% in educational services, health care, and social assistance; 15% in retail trade; 11% in professional, scientific, management, and administrative occupations; 10% in manufacturing; 10% in finance, insurance, and real estate; and 9% in arts, entertainment, recreation, and accommodation. The median family income in 2006 was estimated to be $64,697 according to the American Community Survey. Unemployment in 2006 was 6.1%.

New residents are often attracted to the community because of its strong educational and cultural institutions. Bilingual census reports filed with the Illinois State Board of Education by local schools show that a majority of students speak a language other than English at home including Spanish, Urdu, Assyrian, Russian, Korean, Filipino, Greek, and over eighty other languages. According to the 2006 American Community Survey, 42% of residents were foreign born. English Language Learner courses are offered through Oakton Community College and the Oakton District Public Library Literacy Coalition. Classes are available at the public library, school districts, and some religious institutions as well as at Oakton.

Nearly half the residents have lived in the community for 15 or more years. About 12% changed residence within the past year. About 17% are not citizens. According to the American Community Survey, 23.8% speak English "less than very well." Drawing on its ethnic, religious, and racial diversity, Skokie is a community that is adapting to an ever-changing environment while trying to preserve and promote the best from its past and present.

The library is located in the southwest corner of Skokie, across the Green from the Village Hall. It is on Oakton Street, a major East–West thoroughfare, and near several other principal routes including Lincoln Avenue, Niles Center Road, Skokie Boulevard, and Gross Point Road. Once the heart of downtown Skokie, the Oakton Street business area has experienced considerable change as many of the older specialty shops have moved to shopping malls and other suburban locations. The village and Independent Merchants of Downtown Skokie have targeted Oakton Street for development of new retail sites, residences, facade improvement, and streetscape beautification. Much of this activity is stimulated by the recently initiated new, state-of-the-art Illinois Science and Technology Park in the downtown area, on the site of an abandoned pharmaceutical research facility. A downtown Skokie Swift stop is planned for construction within the next two years. The nearby Hartstein campus of Oakton Community College has undergone a major expansion to locate all of its technology programs at the Skokie site, serving about 3,000 students per year. The library, as the western anchor of the downtown area, continues to draw people into downtown Skokie.

Carolyn A. Anthony, Director, 6/1996, revised CAA 7/2008

B. Library Description

The Skokie Public Library serves the Village of Skokie, a community of 10.47 square miles situated just north of Chicago, Illinois. The library was founded as a volunteer-supported institution in 1930 and began receiving tax support in 1941. Through 1959, the library functioned in rented quarters. A referendum for construction of a library building was approved in 1958 and an award-winning 34,000 square foot building was opened for service in February 1960. A proposal for a building addition and the construction of a branch library failed in 1965. After a study and the decision to abandon the branch concept, the board of trustees decided to significantly expand the library at the central site. A referendum for this proposal was approved by the voters in December 1969, and the building was expanded to 100,860 square feet in 1972. A renovation was done in 1992. An addition, completed in 2003, including a third floor and expansion of the building to the west, brought the total square footage of the library to 134,000. As part of the library's capital development program, the library acquired property and added 170 dedicated library parking spaces to the west of the building, supplementing the parking on the east side that is shared with Village Hall.

Because the library is not in the physical center of the village, the Bookmobile reaches people, particularly in the northern and eastern parts of the village, for whom a visit to the main library may be more of a trip.

The library offers a range of materials and services to persons of all ages and ethnicities. The library has a book stock of over 425,000 volumes; more than 150,000 compact discs, DVDs, and other items in various audiovisual formats; nearly 900 current periodical subscriptions; and a growing number of electronic books and reference databases. With 42% of Skokie residents foreign born according to the 2006 American Community Survey, and 90 languages other than English spoken in the homes of Skokie school children, the library maintains collections in more than a dozen languages including Russian, Spanish, Korean, Chinese, Urdu, and Gujarati, among others. The community relies on the library for a supply of current popular materials in many formats and languages. It is one of the largest libraries in the North Suburban Library System (NSLS), a cooperative multitype library system of more than 650 members. The NSLS provides van delivery between libraries, a variety of continuing education programs, consortial purchasing programs, and consulting assistance with technology and other library-related concerns. The NSLS also facilitates communication among staff in member libraries through electronic communities of practice and forums for staff interest groups. Public libraries in the NSLS permit reciprocal borrowing of most library materials by residents of other NSLS communities. While many public libraries in the NSLS also allow residents of public libraries in other Illinois library systems to borrow materials, the Skokie Public Library does not presently extend reciprocal borrowing privileges to residents in library systems other than the NSLS.

Just as the library building and Bookmobile make the library's physical resources available to patrons, the library's online resources make library services available to busy patrons who need access from any place, at any time, every day of the year. Some patrons may experience the library only through our online presence, and the library strives to make its online service options efficient self-service tools for finding and using information. The online services are focused on and relevant to the Skokie community and support fulfillment of the library's mission, goals, and objectives.

As the Web has evolved over the past 15 years or so, the library has focused on developing and continually improving a comprehensive library website and SkokieNet (www.skokienet.org), the library's community website. Selected Web resources are catalogued for integrated access through the library catalog. A number of online databases provide authoritative information, much of which can be accessed from home or office at any time. The library also provides access to an increasing number of books in electronic format and to downloadable audiobooks. As the Web continues to evolve, the library is paying increasing attention to deepening the involvement of online patrons with the library by evaluating and increasing the library's presence in other online venues such as including social media and through the use of various online communication tools such as instant messaging. In addition to the ever-changing Web-based resources, the library makes use of other Internet "push" technologies, such as e-mail and RSS feeds, to increase awareness of library resources and to deliver information to patrons.

Access to the Skokie Public Library's collection is provided by an integrated automation system, with direct links to the collections of other area libraries that use Innovative Interfaces as well as a connection to OCLC WorldCat. The library offers more than 65 electronic databases, many of which can be accessed remotely through the library's website. The website also features downloadable e-books, audiobooks, and films; digitized local historical materials; staff-developed indexes to local newspapers; recommendations for reading; reviews of materials for adults and children; a calendar of events at the library; and links to other resources. Both the library's website and SkokieNet, the library's community-information database, receive more than one million hits each year. Internet access is offered from about 90 public computers in Adult and Youth Services. A wireless network provides Internet access to persons using their own laptops or one of the library laptops available for use within the building.

Circulation of library materials in FY 2008 was 1,625,000, representing nearly 24 items per capita. About 14% of the circulation was by reciprocal borrowers from other library service areas. Information Desk statistics for 2008 were 232,000 for a per-capita volume of 3.4. the Skokie Public Library built a strong reference collection and service over the years; this service was augmented by online searching of remote computerized databases in 1987 and by Internet access in 1995. Because of its established reputation for reference, the library's volume of reference transactions has continued to be relatively strong despite widespread and growing use of the Internet by the public. Nonetheless, the volume of reference transactions has dropped 14% in the last two years while there has been an increase in Internet reference. Staff members are proud of providing a high level of personalized service to the public, and the community has indicated that this service level is expected and appreciated.

The community has also come to expect an abundance and variety of library programs. Attendance at library programming has been increasing as well as use of library meeting rooms by the public. The building was designed to encompass the role of cultural center as well as more traditional library functions. A large, open lobby features ideal exhibition space for art on the walls or freestanding exhibits while a smaller reception area outside the meeting rooms provides a more intimate setting for exhibits of photography and graphic arts. Concerts, dance performances, lectures, and movies are presented in the Petty Auditorium, a facility that seats up to 200 people, equipped with a stage, projection booth, theater lights, and an excellent sound system including an FM system for the hearing impaired. Next door to the Petty, the Mary Radmacher Meeting Room on the first floor is used for lectures, English and literacy classes, cooking demonstrations, smaller film showings, and other library programs, as well as accommodating an overflow crowd from the Petty for viewing a popular presenter via video. A third meeting room on the main floor is used for book discussions and other smaller gatherings. All of the meeting areas are also reserved by community groups for their meetings and activities. For young people, there is a children's story room in the Youth Services Department for storytimes, films, puppet shows, and other kids' programs, and also a craft room for group programs and use by visitors who pick up simple craft supplies from the service desk. Separate computer labs for adults and youth segregate Internet usage and allow for scheduled group instruction. Several specially equipped computers have large print, voice, or Braille output for use by the visually impaired and other assistive devices for children with special needs. With the help of Library Services and Technology Act (LSTA) grant funds, the library has endeavored to make all services as accessible as possible to persons with hearing or vision impairment and also to those who are mobility limited or have other special needs. Outreach programs are taken to

the community through the coordination of Community Services. The library offers 133 hours of programming per week on cable channel 24, a dedicated library channel received by Skokie cable subscribers through two different cable providers. A calendar of library events, exhibits, and programs is published four times per year and distributed to every household in Skokie. The library's events are listed in the village newsletter, *NEWSKOKIE*, which is mailed to homes ten times per year.

Because of the degree of change in the community, the library has initiated a more proactive marketing plan in recent years. All new residents receive a welcome letter and invitation to an open house or tour. More than 20% have responded and signed up for cards. When people sign up for a library card or renew their privileges, they have the option of giving us their e-mail address to receive targeted, brief notices of twelve different types of programs and highlighted new fiction, nonfiction, or genre titles of their choice. Youth Services also initiated an online newsletter for K–8 teachers. New flyers featuring more images than text invite people to "Learn at the Library" or "Relax at the Library" and are distributed at community festivals and events.

With 42% of residents foreign born and 58% speaking a language other than English at home, the library has taken a number of steps to accommodate residents and facilitate library use. Colorful banners on light poles along the street and in the parking lot read "Library" in many languages. The word "Welcome" appears in many languages in a frieze in the vestibule of each library entrance and also on the first screen of the library's website. Machine translations of the website are available in five different languages. Portal screens with custom translation are posted in Spanish, Russian, and Korean, outlining library services such as foreign newspapers and databases of interest to native language speakers. Library staff participate in PolyTalk, a statewide program that makes translators available to library users throughout the state. The library seeks staff with foreign-language proficiency. We have librarians speaking Russian, Spanish, and Korean, with other languages covered by support staff.

Library directions and improved signage help people navigate within the library. To facilitate use of a large and potentially daunting nonfiction collection, browsing display units feature titles face out in 24 categories. Alternate stacks feature face-out titles on the stack end while others feature large images denoting the subject covered such as "cooking."

To bring newer residents into the library, a citizenship class is offered as well as two different sessions of adult learning. An aide to the area congresswoman is in the library two evenings per month to assist people with matters concerning immigration, social security, veterans' benefits, Medicare, and other Federal programs. Both support for the library and use by the community is strong. More than half of community residents are registered for library cards. The gate count for FY 2008 indicated that the average Skokian visited the library 11 times in the year. A challenge for the library is to continually adapt the mix of materials and services to meet the needs of a constantly changing, increasingly diverse community.

Carolyn A. Anthony, Director, 7/2008

C. Resources Selection Policy

The Skokie Public Library board of trustees has adopted the following resources selection policy to guide librarians and to inform the public about the principles upon which selections are made.

1. Mission Statement

The mission statement of the library guides the selection of materials as it does the development of services and the allocation of resources:

> The Skokie Public Library promotes lifelong learning, discovery, and enrichment through a broad spectrum of materials, technologies, and experiences. Serving a diverse population, the library facilitates access to information, the exchange of ideas, and the building of community.

The library supports the individual's right to have access to ideas and information representing all points of view. The board of trustees has adopted the American Library Association's "Library Bill of Rights," "Freedom to Read," and "Freedom to View," statements, attached herewith.

2. Objectives

The library acquires and makes available materials that inform, educate, entertain, and enrich persons as individuals and as members of society. Since no library can possibly acquire all print and nonprint materials, every library must of necessity employ a policy of selectivity in acquisitions. The library provides, within its financial limitations, a general collection of reliable materials embracing broad areas of knowledge. Included are works of enduring value and timely materials on current issues. Within the framework of these broad objectives, selection is made on the basis of community needs, both those expressed and those inferred from study of community demographics and evidence of areas of interest. Consideration is given to reference and circulating materials for adults and young people.

Other community resources and area library resources are considered in selecting materials. The library is a member of the North Suburban Library System, a multitype system of more than 645 academic, school, special, and public libraries in Cook, Kane, Lake, and McHenry Counties. Skokie Public Library cardholders have access to materials in these libraries. Through interlibrary loan agreements, librarians may obtain for patrons of the library materials from libraries in Chicago, throughout the state of Illinois, and throughout the United States. Other information may be obtained through electronic access of remote databases including numerous specialized and technical resources. License agreements enable the library to make available a variety of e-books, digital audiobooks, e-videos, and music materials.

New formats shall be considered for the circulating collection when—by industry report, national survey results, and evidence from local requests—a significant portion of the community population has the necessary technology to make use of the format. Availability of items in the format, the cost per item, and the library's ability to acquire and handle the items will also be factors in determining when a new format will be collected. Similar considerations will influence the decision to delete a format from the library's collections.

Impartiality and judicious selection shall be exercised in all materials acquisition practices. Allocation of the materials budget and the number of items purchased for each area of the collection will be determined by indicators of use, the average cost per item, and objectives for development of the collection as expressed in the library's *Collection Development and Resources Access Plan*.

3. Responsibility for Selection

Ultimate responsibility for materials selection rests with the director, who operates within the framework of policies determined by the board of trustees. All professional staff members may participate in the selection of library materials. The department heads ensure that selectors' choices reflect the resources selection policy and collection development plan of the library. A coordinator of collection development oversees the selection process, making appropriate selection tools available and tracking the materials budget by selector to ensure a flow of new materials throughout the year according to budget allocation.

4. Methods for Selection

Selection is a discerning and interpretive process that involves general knowledge of the subject and its important literature, familiarity with the materials in the collection, awareness of the bibliographies of the subject, and recognition of the needs of the community. Materials are judged on the basis of the content and style of the work as a whole, not by selected portions or passages. Among standard criteria applied are literary merit, enduring value, accuracy, authoritativeness, social significance, importance of subject matter to the collection, soundness of the author's attitude and approach, cost, scarcity of material on the subject, and availability elsewhere. Quality and suitability of the format are also considered. Specific considerations for each area of the collection are noted in the collection development plan.

Tools used in selection include professional journals, trade journals, online resources, subject bibliographies, publishers' promotional materials, and reviews from reputable sources. Purchase suggestions from patrons are welcome and are given serious consideration.

Materials are selected to meet the objectives of public library service. Because the library serves a community embracing a wide range of ages, ethnic backgrounds, educational levels, and interests, the library may fulfill a number of roles in the community.

The library does not attempt to meet curriculum needs of education programs at any level, although a variety of complementary and supplementary resources are provided. Textbooks are acquired if they serve the general public by providing information on subjects where little or no material is available in any other form. In selecting materials for the collection, librarians will consider general educational, commercial, cultural, and civic enterprises of individuals and organizations within the community.

5. Weeding

To maintain an up-to-date, useful collection, worn and obsolete materials are continuously weeded. Materials may also be withdrawn if they are little used or superseded by a new edition or better work on the same subject. Depth and breadth of varying degrees are desirable in various areas of the collection. The collection development plan serves as a guide for weeding and maintaining the collection as well as for the selection of materials.

6. Gifts

Gifts of books and other library materials are accepted by the library with the understanding that they will be considered for addition to the collection in accordance with the resources selection policy. Gifts of more than one hundred items or items over five years old should be discussed with a librarian in advance to determine if the items will be useful to the collection. The library reserves the right to sell or otherwise dispose of gift materials not added to the collection.

Gifts of funds are always welcome. Recommendations from the donor are honored if they are in accord with the resources selection policy. (See section H, "Gift Book Policy")

7. Reconsideration of Library Resources

A singular obligation of the public library is to reflect within its collection differing points of view on controversial or debatable subjects. The library does not promulgate particular beliefs or views, nor does the selection of an item express or imply endorsement of the viewpoint of the author. Library materials will not be marked or identified to show approval or disapproval of the contents, nor will items be sequestered, except for the purpose of protecting them from damage or theft.

Comments from members of the community about the collection or individual items in the collection frequently provide librarians with useful information about interests or needs that may not be adequately met by the collection. The library welcomes expression of opinion by patrons, but will be governed by this resources selection policy in making additions to or deleting items from the collection.

Patrons who request the reconsideration of library materials may be asked to put their request in writing by completing and signing the form appended to this policy, entitled "Request for Reconsideration of Library Material."

Upon receipt of a formal, written request, the director will appoint an ad hoc committee from the professional staff including, but not limited to, the selector for the subject area of the item in question and the appropriate department head. The committee will make a written recommendation to the director who will then make a decision regarding the disposition of the material. The director will communicate this decision and the reasons for it in writing to the person who initiated the request for reconsideration at the earliest possible date. The director will inform the board of trustees of all requests for reconsideration of library materials and their disposition.

In the event that the person who initiated the request is not satisfied with the decision of the director, he or she may appeal for a hearing before the board of trustees by making a written request to the president of the board. If a hearing is granted, the individual will be notified when he or she may address the board. The board of trustees reserves the right to limit the length of presentation and number of speakers at the hearing.

The board will determine whether the request for reconsideration has been handled in accordance with stated policies and procedures of the library. On the basis of this determination, the board may vote to uphold or override the decision of the director.

Adopted by the Skokie Public Library Board of Library Trustees 2/21/90; Reviewed 2/13/08.

D. Request for Reconsideration of Library Material

Author: _____

Title: _____ Format: _____

      Publisher: _____ Publication Date: _____

Request initiated by: _____

      Address: _____ City: _____

      Zip Code: _____ Phone: _____

Is this request made on behalf of:

    _____ Yourself

    _____ Organization _____ (Name of Organization)

Have you read/viewed this title in its entirety? _____

What is your objection to the resource? (Please be specific; i.e., cite pages.) _____

_____

Is there anything positive about the material? _____

_____

Please state the reason for your request _____

_____

_____

Action Requested:

    _____

    _____

Have you read the Skokie Public Library resources selection policy? _____

Are you aware of the judgment of this material by literary critics or area subject specialists? _____

(Please provide names of reviewers and citations for reviews, if known)

_____

_____

Can you recommend material of comparable literary quality or another title that would convey the

same perspective of the subject created? _____

Date: _____ Signature of Patron: _____

Date: _____ Received by Staff Member: _____

E. Library Bill of Rights

The American Library Association affirms that all libraries are forums for information and ideas, and that the following basic policies should guide their services.

1. Books and other library resources should be provided for the interest, information, and enlightenment of all people of the community the library serves. Materials should not be excluded because of the origin, background, or views of those contributing to their creation.
2. Libraries should provide materials and information presenting all points of view on current and historical issues. Materials should not be proscribed or removed because of partisan or doctrinal disapproval.
3. Libraries should challenge censorship in the fulfillment of their responsibility to provide information and enlightenment.
4. Libraries should cooperate with all persons and groups concerned with resisting abridgment of free expression and free access to ideas.
5. A person's right to use a library should not be denied or abridged because of origin, age, background, or views.
6. Libraries which make exhibit spaces and meeting rooms available to the public they serve should make such facilities available on an equitable basis, regardless of the beliefs or affiliations of individuals or groups requesting their use.

Adopted June 18, 1948.

Amended February 2, 1961, June 27, 1967, and January 23, 1980 by the ALA Council; inclusion of "age" reaffirmed January 24, 1996.

Adopted by the Skokie Public Library Board of Library Trustees 2/21/90; Revised 7/10/96; Reviewed 5/20/98.

F. The Freedom to Read

The freedom to read is essential to our democracy. It is continuously under attack. Private groups and public authorities in various parts of the country are working to remove or limit access to reading materials, to censor content in schools, to label "controversial" views, to distribute lists of "objectionable" books or authors, and to purge libraries. These actions apparently rise from a view that our national tradition of free expression is no longer valid; that censorship and suppression are needed to counter threats to safety or national security, as well as to avoid the subversion of politics and the corruption of morals. We, as individuals devoted to reading and as librarians and publishers responsible for disseminating ideas, wish to assert the public interest in the preservation of the freedom to read.

Most attempts at suppression rest on a denial of the fundamental premise of democracy: that the ordinary individual, by exercising critical judgment, will select the good and reject the bad. We trust Americans to recognize propaganda and misinformation, and to make their own decisions about what they read and believe. We do not believe they are prepared to sacrifice their heritage of a free press in order to be "protected" against what others think may be bad for them. We believe they still favor free enterprise in ideas and expression.

These efforts at suppression are related to a larger pattern of pressures being brought against education, the press, art and images, films, broadcast media, and the Internet. The problem is not only one of actual censorship. The shadow of fear cast by these pressures leads, we suspect, to an even larger voluntary curtailment of expression by those who seek to avoid controversy or unwelcome scrutiny by government officials.

Such pressure toward conformity is perhaps natural to a time of accelerated change. And yet suppression is never more dangerous than in such a time of social tension. Freedom has given the United States the elasticity to endure strain. Freedom keeps open the path of novel and creative solutions, and enables change to come by choice. Every silencing of a heresy, every enforcement of an orthodoxy, diminishes the toughness and resilience of our society and leaves it the less able to deal with controversy and difference.

Now as always in our history, reading is among our greatest freedoms. The freedom to read and write is almost the only means for making generally available ideas or manners of expression that can initially command only a small audience. The written word is the natural medium for the new idea and the untried voice from which come the original contributions to social growth. It is essential to the extended discussion that serious thought requires, and to the accumulation of knowledge and ideas into organized collections.

We believe that free communication is essential to the preservation of a free society and a creative culture. We believe that these pressures toward conformity present the danger of limiting the range and variety of inquiry and expression on which our democracy and our culture depend. We believe that every American community must jealously guard the freedom to publish and to circulate, in order to preserve its own freedom to read. We believe that publishers and librarians have a profound responsibility to give validity to that freedom to read by making it possible for the readers to choose freely from a variety of offerings.

The freedom to read is guaranteed by the Constitution. Those with faith in free people will stand firm on these constitutional guarantees of essential rights and will exercise the responsibilities that accompany these rights.

We therefore affirm these propositions:

1. *It is in the public interest for publishers and librarians to make available the widest diversity of views and expressions, including those that are unorthodox, unpopular, or considered dangerous by the majority.*

   Creative thought is by definition new, and what is new is different. The bearer of every new thought is a rebel until that idea is refined and tested. Totalitarian systems attempt to maintain themselves in power by the ruthless suppression of any concept that challenges the established orthodoxy. The power of a democratic system to adapt to change is vastly strengthened by the freedom of its citizens to choose widely from among conflicting opinions offered freely to them. To stifle every nonconformist idea at birth would mark the end of the democratic process. Furthermore, only through the constant activity of weighing and selecting can the democratic mind attain the strength demanded by times like these. We need to know not only what we believe but why we believe it.

2. *Publishers, librarians, and booksellers do not need to endorse every idea or presentation they make available. It would conflict with the public interest for them to establish their own political, moral, or aesthetic views as a standard for determining what should be published or circulated.*

   Publishers and librarians serve the educational process by helping to make available knowledge and ideas required for the growth of the mind and the increase of learning. They do not foster education by imposing as mentors the patterns of their own thought. The people should have the freedom to read and consider a broader range of ideas than those that may be held by any single librarian or publisher or government or church. It is wrong that what one can read should be confined to what another thinks proper.

3. *It is contrary to the public interest for publishers or librarians to bar access to writings on the basis of the personal history or political affiliations of the author.*

No art or literature can flourish if it is to be measured by the political views or private lives of its creators. No society of free people can flourish that draws up lists of writers to whom it will not listen, whatever they may have to say.

4. *There is no place in our society for efforts to coerce the taste of others, to confine adults to the reading matter deemed suitable for adolescents, or to inhibit the efforts of writers to achieve artistic expression.*

To some, much of modern expression is shocking. But is not much of life itself shocking? We cut off literature at the source if we prevent writers from dealing with the stuff of life. Parents and teachers have a responsibility to prepare the young to meet the diversity of experiences in life to which they will be exposed, as they have a responsibility to help them learn to think critically for themselves. These are affirmative responsibilities, not to be discharged simply by preventing them from reading works for which they are not yet prepared. In these matters values differ, and values cannot be legislated; nor can machinery be devised that will suit the demands of one group without limiting the freedom of others.

5. *It is not in the public interest to force a reader to accept the prejudgment of a label characterizing any expression or its author as subversive or dangerous.*

The ideal of labeling presupposes the existence of individuals or groups with wisdom to determine by authority what is good or bad for others. It presupposes that individuals must be directed in making up their minds about the ideas they examine. But Americans do not need others to do their thinking for them.

6. *It is the responsibility of publishers and librarians, as guardians of the people's freedom to read, to contest encroachments upon that freedom by individuals or groups seeking to impose their own standards or tastes upon the community at large; and by the government whenever it seeks to reduce or deny public access to public information.*

It is inevitable in the give and take of the democratic process that the political, the moral, or the aesthetic concepts of an individual or group will occasionally collide with those of another individual or group. In a free society individuals are free to determine for themselves what they wish to read, and each group is free to determine what it will recommend to its freely associated members. But no group has the right to take the law into its own hands, and to impose its own concept of politics or morality upon other members of a democratic society. Freedom is no freedom if it is accorded only to the accepted and the inoffensive. Further, democratic societies are more safe, free, and creative when the free flow of public information is not restricted by governmental prerogative or self-censorship.

7. *It is the responsibility of publishers and librarians to give full meaning to the freedom to read by providing books that enrich the quality and diversity of thought and expression. By the exercise of this affirmative responsibility, they can demonstrate that the answer to a "bad" book is a good one, the answer to a "bad" idea is a good one.*

The freedom to read is of little consequence when the reader cannot obtain matter fit for that reader's purpose. What is needed is not only the absence of restraint, but the positive provision of opportunity for the people to read the best that has been thought and said. Books are the major channel by which the intellectual inheritance is handed down, and the principal means of its testing and growth. The defense of the freedom to read requires of all publishers and librarians the utmost of their faculties, and deserves of all Americans the fullest of their support.

We state these propositions neither lightly nor as easy generalizations. We here stake out a lofty claim for the value of the written word. We do so because we believe that it is possessed of enormous variety and usefulness, worthy of cherishing and keeping free. We realize that the application of these propositions may mean the dissemination of ideas and manners of expression that are repugnant to many persons. We do not state these propositions in the comfortable belief that what people read is unimportant. We believe rather that what people read is deeply important; that ideas can be dangerous; but that the suppression of ideas is fatal to a democratic society. Freedom itself is a dangerous way of life, but it is ours.

This statement was originally issued in May of 1953 by the Westchester Conference of the American Library Association and the American Book Publishers Council, which in 1970 consolidated with the American Educational Publishers Institute to become the Association of American Publishers.

Adopted June 25, 1953, by the ALA Council and the AAP Freedom to Read Committee; amended January 28, 1972; January 16, 1991; July 12, 2000; June 30, 2004.

Adopted by the Skokie Public Library Board of Library Trustees 2/21/90; Revised 4/95; 7/10/96; Reviewed 5/20/98; Reviewed 3/9/2005.

G. Freedom to View

The freedom to view, along with the freedom to speak, to hear, and to read, is protected by the First Amendment to the Constitution of the United States. In a free society, there is no place for censorship of any medium of expression. Therefore these principles are affirmed:

1. To provide the broadest possible access to film, video, and other audiovisual materials because they are a means for the communication of ideas. Liberty of circulation is essential to insure the constitutional guarantee of freedom of expression.
2. To protect the confidentiality of all individuals and institutions using film, video, and other audiovisual materials.
3. To provide film, video, and other audiovisual materials which represent a diversity of views and expression. Selection of a work does not constitute or imply agreement with or approval of the content.
4. To provide a diversity of viewpoints without the constraint of labeling or prejudging film, video, and other audiovisual materials on the basis of the moral, religious, or political beliefs of the producer or filmmaker or on the basis of controversial content.
5. To contest vigorously, by all lawful means, every encroachment upon the public's freedom to view.

This statement was originally drafted by the Freedom to View Committee of the American Film and Video Association (formerly the Educational Film Library Association) and was adopted by the AFVA Board of Directors in February 1979. This statement was updated and approved by the AFVA Board of Directors in 1989.

Adopted by the Skokie Public Library Board of Library Trustees 2/21/90; Revised 7/10/96; Reviewed 5/20/98.

H. Gift Book Policy

When a patron offers to give books, magazines, or audiovisual materials to the library, the following guidelines apply. If there is a question about these guidelines or a special situation, the patron should be referred to the librarian in charge of donated materials or to the coordinator of Collection Development.

We will accept up to one hundred hardcover and paperback books and audiovisual materials. All items should be in very good condition. Nothing that is marked in, yellowing, musty, or damaged will be accepted.

We will not take anything over five years old in these categories: accounting, computer science, economics, medicine, and science. We will accept editions of standard encyclopedias.

No textbooks will be accepted.

Magazines will not be accepted.

Local history materials from the Chicago and Skokie areas are welcome, as are foreign-language materials.

The donor will receive a written acknowledgement of his or her gift if desired. Please take name and address and the number of books if the patron would like it to be mentioned. Library staff will not appraise the books or indicate a value in the acknowledgement letter. The donor may request that a gift plate be affixed to new books.

The library reserves the right to use donated materials as the staff sees fit.

Approved August 2, 1989, by the Skokie Public Library Board of Trustees

III. COLLECTION DEVELOPMENT AND RESOURCES ACCESS PLAN

(Procedures and Guidelines)

A. Library Mission Statement

The Skokie Public Library promotes lifelong learning, discovery, and enrichment through a broad spectrum of materials, technologies, and experiences. Serving a diverse population, the library facilitates access to information, the exchange of ideas, and the building of community.

B. Resource Development Goals

The Skokie Public Library will provide resources, including materials and electronic access to information, which meet patrons' interests and needs in a timely, cost-effective manner.

The library will provide a broadly based and diverse collection of resources that can support the library's mission and roles in the community, currently emphasizing developing the community workforce, early literacy for toddlers and preschoolers, helping teens develop and parents assist in that development, support for small business, resources for local information, and bridging the digital divide.

The library will strive to provide a balance of viewpoints on all subjects through its collections and access to resources in multiple formats.

The library will purchase current materials and provide access to electronic resources proportionate to levels of demand and use, taking care to anticipate and respond to indications of significant new needs.

To maintain the vitality of library resources, staff will practice ongoing collection management, using output measures, circulation reports, software application monitoring reports, and other data for continuous collection evaluation. Worn, damaged, obsolete, and dated materials will be weeded from the collection on a regular basis.

Resources in any format that fails to meet the needs of our users will be discontinued.

The library will keep abreast of technological changes that affect the development of the collection and resources.

The library will develop its collection and resources with an awareness of the resources available in surrounding libraries and organizations.

The library recognizes its responsibility in the development of shared resources within the North Suburban Library System as well as its immediate community. The library will continue to participate in cooperative acquisitions programs, maintaining regional public library resource collections, and participating in the creation and maintenance of shared access to benefit the community as well as residents throughout the North Suburban Library System area.

The library encourages and at all times welcomes patron suggestions, comments, and ideas about the collection and resources.

The collection will not grow larger than its current size, although parts of the collection may grow in response to community interests and needs, while other parts decrease in size because of lessened patron interest or format obsolescence.

C. A. Anthony
7/1996, 2/2008

C. Resource Selection and Organization

1. Selection Organization

Ultimate responsibility for resource selection rests with the director, who operates within the framework of policies set by the board of trustees. The director determines the budget, guidelines, and organizational structure for the librarians and paraprofessionals who select resources.

At the Skokie Public Library, the Resource Development Team is responsible for implementing the library's resource development and management program. The coordinator of Collection Development oversees the selection process. The coordinator reports to the associate director of Public Services and works with the associate director and department heads in setting yearly objectives and seeing that they are met. The coordinator of Collection Development also works closely with the assistant director of Technical Services and the supervisor of Circulation Services to see that materials are being processed and available for circulation in a timely and an orderly manner. The coordinator works with all selectors to see that the collection is developed and maintained. The coordinator supervises and trains all librarians and paraprofessionals in the Adult Services Department and the Youth Services Department in areas relating to material selection and collection maintenance. Most full- and part-time professional librarians have selection duties. Paraprofessionals are given selection responsibilities in accordance with their skills and background.

Selectors are responsible for choosing appropriate materials for their areas, maintaining circulation and turnover rates, weeding these areas to keep them current with need and demand, seeing that materials are in good physical condition and replacing them if not, and spending their budget in a timely and organized manner.

2. Selection Criteria

The criteria for the evaluation of resources includes literary or artistic merit, enduring value, accuracy, authoritativeness, timeliness, social significance, popular demand, need for information or materials in an area, availability of these materials elsewhere, and cost. Any or all of these factors are used when selecting resources. In addition, when selecting electronic resources, consideration is given to a user-friendly yet robust search mechanism and compatibility with existent library computer systems. At all times, selectors should choose materials that will build a well-rounded collection that includes all viewpoints and opinions and that will meet patrons' needs and demands. In addition to circulation statistics, the following direct and indirect indicators of patrons' interests are also important guides for selection: purchase suggestions, lists

of missing books, books requiring repair or replacement, interlibrary loan requests, and suggestions for additional materials by public desk staff. A well-rounded collection meets most needs of students as well as independent learners; however, the library recognizes that it is a supplementary rather than primary resource for students.

3. Selection Tools

Selection of resources is done from book reviews in professional and popular journals and magazines, subject bibliographies, annual lists of recommended titles, publishers' catalogs, online sources, patron requests, and sales representatives for specific materials. The standard selection tools used by librarians include the following: *Kirkus Reviews, Library Journal, Booklist, Choice, Publishers Weekly, Sound and Vision, Billboard, School Library Journal, Bulletin of the Center for Children's Books, Horn Book, Ingram Advance, Baker and Taylor's Forecast, Kliatt, New York Times Book Review,* and *Chicago Tribune Books.*

4. Standing Orders

Materials that are updated annually or every few years and that are necessary to the collection are put on standing order. The majority of these materials are reference books, but travel books, college guides, test review books, résumé books, and annual literary anthologies are also put on standing order for the circulating collection. The coordinator of Collection Development and the coordinator of Information Services approve additions to the standing order list and review the list on a periodic basis. Materials such as youth paperbacks, readers in series, and Adult Services large type are also purchased on a blanket order plan.

5. Resource Format

Resources are purchased in the most appropriate format for patron use.

Books are generally purchased in hardcover editions because of their durability. However, paperback editions may be purchased, and are preferred in cases where the hardcover edition is extremely expensive and the title either would be used infrequently or is an item that would be weeded from the collection in a few years. Paperbacks are often purchased as added copies of popular titles to meet patron demand and as part of the paperback browsing collection. Library editions are purchased for heavily used titles in the Youth Services Department because of their durability.

Textbooks are purchased in areas where there is little or no material in any other format or where they add substantially to the collection. The library does not buy the textbooks used by the local high schools or community college, regarding it as the responsibility of the school library to provide copies of these course materials for their students. Some local schools provide the library copies of current textbooks so they will be available to students for homework reference.

New formats shall be considered for the circulating collection when—by industry report, national survey results, and evidence from local requests—a significant portion of the community population has the necessary technology to make use of the format. Availability of items in the format, the cost per item, and the library's ability to acquire and handle the items will also be factors in determining when a new format will be collected. Similar considerations will influence the decision to delete a format from the library's collections.

The availability of information in electronic format has allowed the library to expand the breadth and accessibility of its collections. Skokie Public Library cardholders can now access magazine articles, newspapers, books, audiobooks, and music from outside the library at any time. Access to these resources is also available to all from within the library. Electronic resources are added to the library's collection on the basis of utility and popularity. The availability of e-books and databases in areas such as automobile repair and computer technology has ensured that current materials on models and topics, no matter how popular, will be available to our users. In the past, when we were dependent on print materials, books were often checked out or missing at the time of need.

In many cases, specialized reference products that the library has traditionally subscribed to in print are now maintained in electronic format for reasons of currency and enhanced search capabilities.

6. Multiple Copies

While the library does not have the budgetary resources to buy multiple copies of every title it owns, it does buy multiple copies of titles that have high patron demand. It is up to each selector to determine how many copies of a title should be ordered, and in what format. Generally, two copies of titles with broad appeal are ordered. Bestselling authors are purchased in quantities sufficient to meet anticipated patron demand. For titles with many reserves, one book is purchased for every five patron reserves. In subject areas such as résumés and travel books, where the interest is in the subject more than in a particular title, the library prefers to buy one or two copies of several different titles instead of buying numerous copies of one title. The library tries to offer variety and depth through this approach.

7. Rare and Expensive Books

The library believes that materials selected for the circulating collection should be judged on merit and value to

the collection rather than the cost of an item. If an item is expensive (more than $75), the selector will check to see what other materials on the subject we have in the collection, how this new book compares, and the importance of the title to the development of the collection. If the selector decides it is needed, the title will be added to the circulating collection and treated as any other item. If it is lost or damaged, the selector will decide if it should be replaced.

Since the library is a public library whose materials are available to the public, at no time will rare or unusual books that would require special handling be added. If it comes to staff attention that a book already owned has now become exceedingly rare or expensive, the decision will be made on a book-by-book basis whether to keep the item or find an appropriate library or archive that could house the material.

8. Bindery Guidelines

When a book is returned damaged or in poor condition, Circulation staff will send it to Technical Services, where it will be routed for selectors to check.

Selectors should regularly check the shelves in their areas and decide which books should be repaired, rebound, or withdrawn.

In deciding which books should be sent to the bindery, librarians should be very selective. In many cases, it is more cost efficient to buy a replacement or to buy a newer title. This also helps keep the collection looking new.

Rebinding should be reserved for items that cannot be replaced or would be too costly to replace. The following books are usually sent to the bindery unless they are so extensively damaged that they can't be rebound:

- foreign-language books
- out-of-print books that are of high value to the library collection
- one volume of a set that is still in good condition and important to the collection
- expensive books that are important to the collection

Books that cannot be repaired or rebound according to the above guidelines should be withdrawn.

9. Deselection of Materials

Titles are withdrawn from the library's collection through systematic weeding by selectors or because of loss or physical damage. Materials that are withdrawn because of loss or damage are reported to the selectors, who then decide whether the item should be replaced using the same criteria as for selection. Other factors that selectors must consider when deciding on replacements include the number of copies of a title the library owns, the availability of newer materials on the subject, the importance of the work in its field, its listing in standard bibliographies, and its cost. Generally, in any one year, the library will not spend more than ten to fifteen percent of the budget allocated to a collection area on replacement and retrospective purchases. Since books are in print for a relatively short period of time, out-of-print dealers and remainder houses will be used to replace titles considered essential for the collection. While some audiovisual materials that are withdrawn will be replaced with new popular titles, replacement copies of classic titles will be sought.

Systematic evaluation and weeding of the collection is required of every selector in order to keep the collection responsive to patrons' needs, ensure its vitality and usefulness to the community, and make room for newer materials. Guidelines for collection size and expected turnover of titles are determined for each area of the collection. Weeding identifies damaged items, ephemeral materials that are no longer used, out-of-date materials, extra copies that are not being used, and materials that are not appropriate for the collection. Weeding also helps a selector evaluate the collection by identifying areas or titles where additional materials are needed, older editions that need to be updated, and subjects, titles, or authors that are no longer of interest to the community. If a selector is uncertain about a title to be withdrawn, he or she should check standard bibliographic tools in the subject to see if the title has historical or literary value that might merit its being kept. Holdings of other area libraries may also be considered in making deselection decisions. Withdrawn materials that are in good condition will be put in the book sale. No materials will be held for or given to individuals.

See the following for more on weeding:

- Boon, Belinda. *The CREW Method: Expanded Guidelines for Collection Evaluation and Weeding for Small and Medium-Sized Public Libraries.* Austin, Tex.: Texas State Library, 1995.
- Slote, Stanley J. *Weeding Library Collections: Library Weeding Methods.* 4th ed. Englewood, Colo.: Libraries Unlimited, 1997.
- Gwinnett County Public Library. *Weeding Guidelines.* Chicago: PLA, 1998.

10. Evaluation of the Resources

The collection needs continuous evaluation to be sure that the library is fulfilling its mission to provide resources in a timely manner that meets patrons' interests and needs. Statistical tools such as circulation reports, collection turnover rates, document delivery studies, fill rates, reference fill rates, shelf allotments, volume counts, and application metering reports on electronic resources are studied to determine how the collection is being used and how it should change to answer patron usage. The collection's holdings are also checked against standard bibliographies and recommended lists to be sure that the library is acquiring recommended materials. The materials themselves are looked at for their physical condition and their use. Finally, patron input and community surveys are also used in evaluating the collection. Through ongoing quantitative and qualitative methods, the director, coordinator of Collection Development, associate director, department heads, and selectors monitor the collection to see that it is serving its public.

D. The Library's Web Presence

1. Purpose and Scope of the Library Website

Description of the Site

The Skokie Public Library website is one of the primary ways that residents of Skokie and the broader community come into contact and interact with the library, both remotely and while in the library building. It promotes awareness and enhances the usefulness of programs, services, and resources in the physical library and provides convenient access to electronic resources including the library catalog, external websites, premium databases subscribed to by the library, and library-created content such as booklists, digital collections, databases, and community information through links to SkokieNet (www.skokienet.org), the library's community website. Library staff members integrate this information in an orderly and intuitive fashion and provide annotations and guides to increase the usefulness to patrons. Most website content resides on one of six major sections (Kids, Movies and Music, Programs, Reading, Research, and Teens). Section coordinators are primarily responsible for selecting and maintaining content for their own sections.

Factors Influencing Site Development

The library website is used both by staff in fulfilling the mission of the library and its departments and by library site users who reflect the cultural, ethnic, linguistic, educational, and generational diversity and trends of the Skokie population. The site is used both within the library and remotely. New interactive technologies are incorporated when beneficial to our users and their interests. Website content is created or selected to promote the library's mission, goals, and objectives and is reviewed regularly for continued relevance and accuracy.

Content Selection Criteria

Websites, subscription databases, and other Web content are selected or created to enhance the usability of the library's print collections; supplement these collections with electronic content; enable patrons and staff to interact, exchange information, and perform library-related tasks; and otherwise serve the library's mission of promoting lifelong learning and access to information, the exchange of ideas, and building of community. The coordinator of Information Services selects subscription databases on the basis of criteria including issues of cost relative to use; the availability of remote access and full-text content; and database maintenance, frequency of updates, and ease of use. Section coordinators select external websites and other content for their sections with the following evaluation criteria:

- Site maintenance. External sites should contain current information and URLs that work and should be reliably accessible.
- Authority. Sites should provide information from clearly identified, authoritative sources.
- Navigation. Complex sites should contain robust yet user-friendly search mechanisms.
- Quality. Sites should represent the best in their field when multiple websites perform similar functions.

Duplication of content on the library website and SkokieNet is to be avoided. Websites for Skokie businesses, services, organizations, educational offerings, and events are included as part of the SkokieNet website rather than the library website, although the library website may include links to relevant sections of SkokieNet where necessary. (Likewise, SkokieNet may also provide links to content on the library website when necessary.) External or library-created websites and other Web content related to Skokie (such as its history, demographics, businesses, services and the like) reside on the SkokieNet website, although the library website may include links to relevant sections of SkokieNet.

Site Maintenance (Retention and Weeding)

All website content is checked regularly by section coordinators for currency and relevance. URLs throughout the site are checked vigorously and corrected expeditiously when necessary. Websites that no longer exist or have changed their missions are removed and, if possible, similar websites substituted in their place. Both the library website as a whole and each major section is reviewed regularly with the goal of identifying areas for improvement. Dynamic content relevant to sections is developed and posted regularly on the opening section pages. The website development coordinator produces statistical reports to monitor site and database usage and identify popular areas. In addition, the website development coordinator produces monthly reports identifying broken links on the various sections of the website. The section coordinators are responsible for verifying these links and making appropriate changes and substitutions when necessary. The website as a whole will be periodically tested by library users to identify problems with site navigation and design.

Continued Development Objectives

The ever increasing amount of content on the Web means that the library website may continue to grow in size. It is important that staff keep abreast of new developments in Web design and technology and incorporate these developments where and when appropriate on the website including means to increase opportunities for patrons to discover resources not specifically sought, provide feedback and post information online, continue to develop more ways patrons can perform library-related tasks online, decrease barriers between patrons and the information contained in databases, and to provide patrons with greater access to the information most relevant to their own needs. In addition, staff will add more Web content in foreign languages to the website to reflect the linguistic diversity of the Skokie population.

2. Purpose and Scope of SkokieNet, the Library's Community Website

Description of the Site

SkokieNet provides access to local information, both within the library and remotely. The SkokieNet manager, assisted by members of the SkokieNet Committee, enables Skokie community agencies and organizations to create and maintain a presence on the Internet. Providing this presence for agencies and organizations allows the opportunity for developing partnerships with community entities, increasing the visibility of the library in the community and enhancing the provision of information unique to Skokie. Links are provided to the webpages of Skokie businesses. In the interest of providing an online reflection of the Skokie community, SkokieNet also functions as a venue for user-generated content. Visitors to SkokieNet may submit stories, photos, and events that they wish to share with the Skokie community at large. This function was previously served by the SkokieTalk website, which SkokieNet absorbed during its most recent redesign.

Content on SkokieNet is organized under sixteen categories: Arts and Entertainment, Business, Clubs and Organizations, Community Calendar, Demographic Information, Education, Government and Politics, Health and Medicine, Libraries, Local Media, Religion, Restaurants and Shopping, Skokie History Center, Social Services, Sports and Recreation, and Transportation and Travel.

Factors Influencing Site Development

SkokieNet is used to find information about the government, history, organizations, businesses, resources, and services of the Skokie community. Website content is created or selected to promote SkokieNet's mission. Because external websites are constantly being created, eliminated, or changed without notice, the SkokieNet manager, assisted by members of the SkokieNet Committee, is vigilant to add or remove external sites and check existing sites to ensure that links are working. All user-generated content, including submitted stories, media, events, and comments, is vetted by the SkokieNet Manager before being made public.

Content Selection Criteria

SkokieNet content is selected to provide the residents of Skokie with information about the Village of Skokie and to enable local agencies, organizations, and businesses to make information about themselves available to the community at large.

The SkokieNet Manager and the members of the SkokieNet Committee select content using the following criteria:

Site maintenance. All pages should contain current information and URLs that both work and are reliably accessible.

Authority. Pages should provide information from clearly identified, authoritative sources.

Navigation. Pages should offer user-friendly search mechanisms.

Quality. When multiple sources of information are available, those selected for inclusion should be the most complete and accurate.

User-generated content submitted to SkokieNet is subject to the same criteria and is approved or rejected on the basis of its relevance to the Skokie community. Any content deemed to contain profane, obscene, libelous, or defamatory remarks is also subject to rejection on the part of the SkokieNet manager.

Duplication of content on SkokieNet and the library website is to be avoided. Websites for Skokie municipal bodies, organizations, businesses, services, and those listing educational offerings and events are included as part of SkokieNet rather than the library website, although the library website may include links to relevant sections of SkokieNet when appropriate. External or library-created websites and other Web content related to Skokie (such as history, demographics, businesses, services, and the like) reside on SkokieNet, although the library website may include links to relevant sections.

Site Maintenance (Retention and Weeding)

All SkokieNet content is checked regularly by the manager and SkokieNet Committee members for currency and relevance. URLs throughout the site are checked vigorously and corrected when necessary. Websites that no longer exist or have changed their missions are removed, and, if possible, similar websites are substituted in their place. SkokieNet content is reviewed regularly by the manager and committee members (and other staff not associated with site development) with the goal of identifying areas for improvement. Dynamic content relevant to the community as a whole is developed and posted on the opening page, and dynamic content relevant to the various categories is developed and posted regularly on the opening category pages. The SkokieNet manager produces statistical reports to monitor site and database usage and identify popular areas. Monthly reports identifying broken links are generated. The SkokieNet manager and committee members are responsible for verifying those links and making appropriate changes and substitutions when necessary. SkokieNet as a whole will be periodically tested by library and community users to identify problems with site navigation and design.

Continued Development Objectives

To maintain SkokieNet in good order, growth will be moderate. Emphasis will be given to adding and updating pages of community agencies and organizations. Links to local businesses will continue to be added and updated.

Member of Skokie's cultural communities will be recruited to create pages highlighting the history and activities of those communities. Those "ethnic" pages already on SkokieNet will be maintained and updated.

Proposed new pages for SkokieNet will be discussed by the SkokieNet Committee. The SkokieNet manager and committee will explore means to increase opportunities for community residents to provide feedback and to post information online, to decrease barriers between residents and the community information they seek, and to provide residents with greater access to the information most relevant to their wants.

E. Definition of Collection Levels

The definitions for collection levels used in this plan have been adapted from the collection levels in the American Library Association's "Guidelines for the Formulation of Collection Development Policies," 1st edition. Since these definitions are designed for academic libraries, they were modified for use with the Skokie Public Library's collection. The definitions were modified to describe the dual nature of public library collections that have materials on subjects that can fit into an academic scheme of learning from introductory through advanced research and also have materials on popular, nontechnical, high-interest subjects that do not readily lend themselves to systematic, hierarchical study. For example, subjects such as logic, chemistry, linguistics, architecture, etc., can be studied in an organized manner that leads the learner from a basic level to a research level of study, and materials can be selected on all of these levels. In contrast, subjects such as cooking, woodworking, fiction, feature films on DVD, etc., are explored in a less structured manner and the materials selected to support this type of use cover a broad spectrum but do not necessarily follow a progression of increasing difficulty wherein knowledge at advanced levels builds on that acquired at foundation levels. In areas such as cooking or woodworking, advanced interest and research levels would include materials for persons employed in the area or involved at the avid hobbyist level. Two different sets of definitions were written as the criteria for defining the adult and youth collections. The following definitions are used by the Adult Services Department.

Basic

A highly selective collection that serves to introduce and define the subject and to indicate the varieties of information available elsewhere. The emphasis is on popular materials and materials that provide a general overview. It includes popular titles, significant works or classics, some major reference works, and a few periodicals in the field. Growth and development are kept at a minimal level.[1]

General Interest and Study

A collection that is adequate to support general interest and initial study; or a popular collection of materials that will have a selection of the important current titles that are consistently weeded. The emphasis is on developing a collection that meets general community needs. It includes a judicious selection from currently published titles supported by selected retrospective significant titles, a broad selection of works of more important writers, a limited selection of the most significant works of secondary writers, a selection of major journals, and current editions of the most significant reference tools and bibliographies pertaining to the subject.

Advanced Interest and Study

A collection that is adequate to support study at post–high school or practitioner levels, or sustained independent study, which is adequate to maintain knowledge of a subject required for student or occupational needs of less-than-research intensity; or a popular collection of materials that has a large and diverse number of titles representing many aspects of the subject and some titles that will be kept for historical value. The emphasis is on developing a comprehensive collection that will support special users in the community but will also cover the needs of a wide range of users. It includes a broad spectrum of current and retrospective materials; complete collections of the works of more important writers, composers, performers, or artists; selections from the works of secondary writers; a selection of representative journals; and new, specialized, and some older reference and bibliographic tools pertaining to the subject.

Beginning Research Level

A collection that includes major published source materials required for independent research or graduate-level study; or a popular collection of materials that is so inclusive and extensive that most works in the area are purchased and retained. The emphasis is on extensive and in-depth coverage of a subject and the development of specialized collections to serve highly specific and specialized portions of the community. Bibliographies, indexes, and databases of a scholarly or technical nature support research by leading to materials both within and outside the scope of the library's collection. Local materials both of general interest and of a unique and specialized nature should be included. User needs at this level are frequently met in whole or part by access to electronic resources.

The following definitions are used by the Youth Services Department.

Basic

A highly selective collection that serves to introduce the varieties of information available. The emphasis is on popular materials and materials that provide a general overview. It includes popular titles as well as significant works or classics. Growth and development are kept at a minimal level.[2]

---

[1] A new collection may be temporarily on a basic level pending further development.

[2] As in Adult Services, a new collection may be temporarily on a basic level pending further development.

General Interest and Study

A collection that is adequate to support general interest and initial study; or a popular collection of materials that will have a strong selection of representative titles. The emphasis is on developing a collection that meets general needs. It includes significant retrospective titles as well as a selection of current titles and is maintained through continuous weeding.

Advanced Interest and Study

A collection that is adequate to support the research and information needs of children through eighth grade; or a popular collection of materials that has a large and diverse number of titles representing many aspects of the subject. Most available works in the area are purchased, very often in multiple copies. A number of representative titles are retained for historical value. Selected young adult and adult titles may be included to provide breadth and depth in a subject area appropriate to the advanced study of youth and beyond the range available in published children's titles.

The depth of a collection is graded on a 1–4 scale, but can be modified by a plus (+) or a minus (-). This allows for greater flexibility in evaluating an area since a minus by a number means that the collection has less breadth (a range of titles at similar level of difficulty with a duplication of titles to meet need), depth (a range of titles at different levels of difficulty), and/or retention of materials than the numerical definition indicates. A plus by a number means that the collection has more breadth, depth, and/or retention of materials than the numerical definition indicates.

In interpreting the assigned collection levels, the full text of the collection descriptions should be read.

The ranking of the collections on three levels—past, current, and future—was adapted from the Pacific Northwest Conspectus Worksheets, which have two levels for evaluating collection intensity. To show trends it was important to identify at what level the collection had been developed in the past (past development collection level), at what level selection is currently being done (current collection selection level), and at what level the collection should develop to achieve the library's mission (future collection development level).

2/2008

F. Adult Services Department

The Skokie Public Library Adult Services Department serves a primary population of Skokie residents over the age of 14. However, the secondary service group includes adults from many surrounding communities as well as children. Of Skokie's estimated population of 73,921 (American Community Survey 2006), there are 51,761 residents over 14 years of age. The library has about 37,500 registered borrowers, of which about 29,600 are Skokie residents. About 80% of cardholders are adults, although it is recognized that many of these are in fact family cards. About 50 nonresidents per year take advantage of our fee card program to have full library privileges. The library also draws patrons from the entire north suburban area because of its special collections and services. They are entitled to borrow materials from the library under the Reciprocal Borrowing Program of the North Suburban Library System (NSLS).

Aside from traditional library services, the department has the Skokie Accessible Library Services (SALS) program, a very active community outreach and programming service, a bookmobile with nearly 3,000 volumes and 20 stops throughout Skokie, and a number of literary interest groups including a book discussion group that has been hosted by the library since 1962 and the Great Books discussion group that has been meeting at the library since 1958. The SALS program, initially funded through three Library Services and Construction Act (LSCA) grants awarded by the state since its inception in 1985, is designed to make library services accessible to patrons whose disabilities and special needs have traditionally made the use of materials and services in the library difficult. Technology and adaptive equipment have opened many materials and services to use by persons on the continuum of disability. These patrons come from all over the Chicagoland area. This outreach program has been seen as a pilot project for statewide and national service to the disabled.

The Adult Services librarians have built a large and diverse collection that tries to anticipate the needs and demands of its varied patrons. The print reference collection has been heavily weeded in recent years, but retains specialties in business and investment, literature, and Skokie and Illinois history. The library has also had a long-term project of microfilming and indexing all its local newspapers.

The library provides access to electronic information resources useful to students, consumers, job hunters, businesspersons, and researchers. Reference service is available to patrons in a number of ways including through e-mail and the Web. In 1995, with the NSLS, the library pioneered the development of NorthStarNet, a library- and community-wide information service accessible on the Internet designed to provide community information of interest to residents in suburban Cook, Lake, McHenry, and eastern Kane counties in Illinois. The library was honored as one of the 1995 Libraries of the Year by the NSLS in recognition of its contribution in developing SkokieNet. The library also maintains a library website (www.skokielibrary.info) with links to a wide variety of information-rich websites. The library provides access to 65 different databases—some accessible remotely—and has digitized local historical materials.

Starting in the middle of the 1970s, the department developed a collection of English and American Literature as part of the Coordinated Acquisitions Program (CAP) of the NSLS. This collection of original works, criticism, biographies, bibliographies, and reference tools had been developed on a beginning research level. The program no longer exists, but the library remains committed to a more robust collection development level for these areas.

Other important resources within the department are the extensive collection of Judaica and Holocaust books, the Employment Resource Center and related job search books and magazines, a heavily used travel guide section, and a varied collection of fiction and nonfiction books in nineteen different foreign languages. The library has added significantly to this foreign-language collection with the assistance of three Library Services and Technology Act (LSTA) collection development grants since 1988. Holdings also include a popular Literacy and ESL (English as a Second Language) collection. The library is also the only public library in the NSLS to be an Illinois Document Depository, offering use of a substantial collection of materials issued by Illinois agencies.

The Adult Services Department has three service desks: Reference, Readers Services, and Movies, Music, and More, which are staffed by a mix of MLS and paraprofessional staff. Reference transactions—including readers' advisory questions—for 2008 were about 70,000, and another 160,000 information transactions were fielded by staff.

The department has a longstanding commitment to the provision of patron-centered collections, services, and programs. For example, it has added 24 sections of browsing shelves with popular nonfiction grouped by subject, rather than shelved by Dewey number, to meet the needs of browsers. Staff provide high levels of support to assist adult patrons by offering year-round book discussions, community outreach programs, regular technology workshops in the use of the Internet and online databases, and one-on-one assistance in use of library resources. Adult Services staff both participate in and lead local, state, and national continuing education professional activities as part of the library's commitment to continuous training.

2/2008

Description of Adult Services Collection by Classification

SUBJECT: 000-Generalities

Description
Materials on computers and related areas are in great demand. Coverage of general topics in computer science (programming, specific operating systems, software applications, hardware and the Internet) is provided. The library science collection consists of major works in the field that are current, practical materials. In journalism, popular writing manuals and major historical treatments and commentaries on journalism are purchased. Recent editions of standard encyclopedias, Great Books of the Western World, and other standard general works are included in this area.

Influencing Factors
It is not surprising that an educated, affluent community that purchases computers and uses online services at a higher than average rate requires an abundance of current computer-related resources. Library staff comprise the primary audience for current library and information science resources; the secondary audience is area library science students. Local writing groups and students continue to create a steady demand for writing and publishing materials and resources. Since the library has provided public-use computers and peripherals for cardholders to use, popular computer applications such as word processors, spreadsheets, and database managers have been loaded onto these computers. Practical manuals and how-to books on each application are available to computer users. Full Internet access is also available at multiple locations within the library.

Selection Plan
Standard selection tools and online resources are used for the area. Publishers catalogs are also used. Generally, single copies are purchased except for computer and software application manuals, which are ordered in multiple copies as needed. Purchase of time-sensitive materials should be in paperback format.

Retention and Weeding
The computer area, aside from some general and historical overviews, must be very current and should be weeded continuously, retaining few practical materials over five years old. In library science, classical works and current practice materials will be retained. In journalism, demand and current circulation dictate the weeding levels.

Development Plan
The escalating demand for computer-related materials and resources has resulted in a proportionally large array of this type of information in the collection. Because of continued anticipated heavy demand, computer materials and resources will be purchased in multiple copies as needed. Library science classics and current practice sources will continue to be represented in the collection by the most appropriate formats.

	Past Collection Development Level	Current Collection Selection Level	Future Collection Development Level
000-Generalities and Computers	2	3	3
010-Bibliography	2	2-	2-
020-Library and Information Sciences	2	2	2
030-General Encyclopedic Works	2	2+	2+
050-General Serial Publications	2	2+	2+
060-General Organizations	2-	2-	2-
070-Journalism	2	2	2
080-General Collections	2	2	2
090-Manuscripts and Book Rarities	2	2-	1+

SUBJECT: 100-Philosophy and Related Disciplines

Description
The philosophy collection consists of works by and about all major philosophers and philosophies, Western and Eastern, ancient and modern. Subjects covered include metaphysics, epistemology, ethics, logic, and the paranormal. Books on witchcraft, astrology, and the occult are included. Psychology and related materials make up approximately 50% of the 100s. This area of the collection consists of works on the history of psychology, collected and complete works of classic psychologists, secondary sources relating to them, textbooks that cover unique material, and books covering all facets of the subject including numerous works of popular psychology.

Influencing Factors
General readers desire materials for self-education, self-help, and pleasure while students need supplemental materials for their courses. The proximity of university libraries precludes the necessity for development beyond the undergraduate level.

Selection Plan
Standard selection tools and online selection resources are routinely used. Single copies are ordered except for popular items that are purchased in multiple copies, preferably paperback editions. An attempt is made to cover as many aspects of the subject as are available.

Retention and Weeding
Classic works by and about major philosophers and psychologists are retained, although new editions and improved translations are purchased to replace inferior ones. New treatments of philosophical and psychological subjects supersede older ones except those that have historical value. Weeding of extra copies, books in poor condition, and ephemeral authors must be done yearly. Within a three-year cycle a complete reexamination of materials that are infrequently used must be done to maintain space for new books.

Development Plan
New works will be purchased on the basis of originality, quality, and demand. Replacement of missing and worn titles is ongoing.

	Past Collection Development Level	Current Collection Selection Level	Future Collection Development Level
100-Philosophy	2	2	2
110-Metaphysics	2	2	2
120-Epistemology	2	2	2
130-Paranormal Phenomena	2+	2+	2+
140-Specific Philosophical Viewpoints	2	2	2
150-Psychology	3	3	3
160-Logic	2	2	2
170-Ethics	2+	2+	2+
180-Ancient, Medieval, Oriental	2+	2+	2+
190-Modern Western Philosophy	2+	2+	2+

SUBJECT: 200-Religion

Description

The religion collection consists of works on the history of world religions, sacred texts, and commentaries of all major religions, doctrinal theological works, and moral and devotional literature. Books on new age and modern religious groups including cults are also included. A large portion of the 200s comprises an in-depth collection of Judaica and Old and New Testament studies.

Influencing Factors

Although decreasing in recent years, the community has a Jewish population that is interested in all topics relating to Judaism. The proximity of specialized collections of Judaica at Hebrew Theological Seminary and Spertus College preclude the necessity of purchasing highly scholarly works in this area. The earliest settlers in Skokie were from Luxembourg and Germany, and their Catholic and Lutheran descendents are still numerous. A factor in the community is the Asian, Middle Eastern, and East Indian populations with a corresponding increase in interest in Islam, Hinduism, and Buddhism. Students from nearby Catholic, Lutheran, and Jewish schools use the collection for course-related work.

Selection Plan

Standard selection tools and online reviewing sources are used regularly. Single copies of titles are ordered except for popular items and books of criticism on the Bible. All religions and denominations are represented as fairly as possible, but sectarian materials of a proselytizing nature may be excluded in favor of unbiased, informative presentations.

Retention and Weeding

Classic works, histories, and sacred texts of major religions and important commentaries are retained. Popular moral and devotional literature and doctrinal theology require up-to-date as well as historical materials. Weeding of extra copies of books in poor condition and books of an ephemeral nature must be done yearly. Within a three-year cycle a complete reexamination of materials that are infrequently used must be done to maintain space for new books.

Development Plan

Replacement of missing and worn titles is ongoing. New titles are added as needed.

	Past Collection Development Level	Current Collection Selection Level	Future Collection Development Level
200-Religion	2	2	2
210-Natural Religion	2	2	2
220-Bible	2+	2+	2+
230-Christian Theology	2	2	2
240-Christian Moral and Devotional	2	2	2
250-Local Church and Religious Orders	2	2	2
260-Social and Ecclesiastical Theology	2	2	2
270-History Of Church	2	2	2
280-Christian Denominations	2	2	2
290–295, 297–299-Other Religions	2	2+	2+
296-Judaica	3	3	2+

SUBJECT: 300-Social Sciences

Description

The social science collection consists of works of recognized authors, historical studies, current theory and interpretation, methodology, some introductory textbooks, and books of popular and advanced interest. One of the most heavily used areas in the social sciences is the economics and commerce area (330s), which covers materials on economic theory, labor, personal finance, stocks and bonds, commodities, options, real estate, and tax preparation. These books range from the introductory level through the advanced level. Another heavily used subject area is social sciences (300s), which includes sociology, anthropology, marriage and the family, ethnic and religious groups, sex roles, aging and retirement, and social interaction. These books also range from the introductory through the advanced level. Materials in the education section (370s) are geared toward parents, students, teachers, and practitioners and include books on the history and philosophy of education, educational psychology, and teaching methods and theory. An extensive collection of career books is also an important part of this area. The social problems area (360s) covers crime, addiction, abuse, health, and environmental issues and contains books for the general reader as well as some materials for human services professionals. In the areas of political science and law and public administration there is an emphasis on American politics and government, citizenship, and law for the lay reader. The final area of the social sciences collection (390s) comprises primarily popular works on costumes, customs, etiquette, holidays, and folklore.

Influencing Factors

The affluence, maturing age, and sophisticated interests of the community strongly influence the selection of materials. A continuing factor in the community is the number of immigrants who need citizenship and educational and vocational materials. High school and college students from Skokie and surrounding communities create a strong demand for assignment-related materials on all levels. The variety of adult education programs in the area has a similar influence.

Selection Plan

To supplement standard selection tools, a variety of publishers' catalogs including those of universities and small presses, and appropriate specialized journals are used on an as-needed basis for all areas of the 300s. Such resources include *Harvard Business Review, Wall Street Journal*, and *Nolo Press*, for example. Standing orders in the 300s include all career titles published by Rosen and VGM. Multiple copies are ordered of books with high interest and demand while single copies of other titles are purchased to give breadth to the collection. Inexpensive paperback editions are chosen over more expensive hardcover editions when they are available.

Retention and Weeding

The social science collection, by virtue of its broad scope and considerable depth, is selectively weeded on an annual basis to remove duplicate copies no longer in demand, out-of-date materials, and books in poor condition. Primary consideration is given to keeping the collection current, but classic authors and historical studies are retained. A complete reexamination of materials that are infrequently used should be done within a three year cycle.

Development Plan

The emphasis is on keeping the collection current and meeting patron demand in high-interest areas. Multiple copies need to be ordered in areas of strong demand.

	Past Collection Development Level	Current Collection Selection Level	Future Collection Development Level
300-Social Sciences	3	3	3
310-Statistics	1	1	1+
320-Political Science	3	3-	3-
330-Economics	3	3	3
340-Law	2+	3	3
350-Public Administration	2	2	2
360-Social Problems and Services	2+	2+	3
370-Education	3	2+	2+
380-Commerce	2	2	2
390-Customs, Etiquette, Folklore	2	2	2+

SUBJECT: Test Collection

Description

The test collection, which is separately shelved and labeled, consists of paperback test preparation books, a few of which include software. These include admissions tests for high school, college, graduate, and professional schools; exams for entrance into the military; placement and equivalency exams; licensing exams for real estate, nursing, commercial driving, and air traffic control; the most popular civil service tests (firefighter, police officer, postal worker, and general civil service worker) and a selection of occupational tests.

Influencing Factors

The high educational attainment goals of the community create a strong demand for academic admissions exam guides. Job hunters and career changers, who frequent the Library in large numbers, need occupational test materials to prepare them for employment.

Selection Plan

Many of the test preparation guides are on standing order. When possible, several different guides are purchased for an exam, thus offering patrons a choice. Multiple copies are ordered as demand indicates. Since test books are published in paperback format, the cost for replacement of lost and outdated items is minimal.

Retention and Weeding

Since these materials are very popular and a good part of the collection may be out at any given time, weeding should be an ongoing process. An earlier edition may be retained along with the current edition to provide more copies of a title, but care must be taken to weed all titles that don't reflect changes in a test's format. It is also important to remember that an older date doesn't necessarily mean an out-of-date title.

Development Plan

The emphasis is on keeping the collection current and providing enough copies to meet patron demand.

	Past Collection Development Level	Current Collection Selection Level	Future Collection Development Level
	3	3	3

SUBJECT: 400-Languages/Linguistics

Description

Standard works in linguistics, circulating dictionaries and books on grammar and usage in English and other languages, and works on Americanisms make up the core of the collection. Emphasis is on the English language, its history, structure, and acquisition. There is a secondary emphasis on foreign-language study materials.

Influencing Factors

The Village of Skokie is an ethnically and racially diverse community with many immigrants. New arrivals from other countries, patrons who plan to travel, and area students rely on the library to offer materials that will help them learn languages.

Selection Plan

Besides the standard selection tools, online sources such as Amazon are consulted. Publications of the university presses are generally available in paperback as well as hardcover, and are purchased in paperback because the hardcover editions tend to be expensive. One copy of each title is generally sufficient, except for dictionaries, phrase books for travelers, and English-language textbooks.

Retention and Weeding

The subject matter of books in the field of languages is stable and not time datable. Books are retained as long as they are in good condition and are meeting the needs of our patrons. Duplicate copies may be weeded to make room for new additions, as may highly specialized texts in linguistics. Within a three-year cycle a complete reexamination of materials that are infrequently used must be done to maintain space for new books.

Development Plan

Patron demand for practical language-learning materials has remained steady. It is important is to replace worn or missing titles, to keep abreast of popular titles, and to monitor demand.

	Past Collection Development Level	Current Collection Selection Level	Future Collection Development Level
400-Language	2	2	2
410-Linguistics	2	2-	2-
420-English Language	2	2+	2+
430-German Language	2-	2-	2-
440-Romance Languages French	2-	3	3
450-Italian, Romanian Languages	2-	3	3
460-Spanish, Portuguese Languages	2-	3	3
470-Italic Languages Latin	1	1	1
480-Hellenic Classical Greek	1	1	1
490-Other Languages	2	3	3

SUBJECT: 500-Pure Sciences

Description

This extensive collection of materials includes the areas of mathematics, astronomy, chemistry, and the life sciences. In addition to the standard disciplines, the philosophy and history of science are covered as well as scientific experiments, how-to books, and popularizations of most scientific subjects. Throughout the area, works range from popular through advanced levels.

Influencing Factors

An interested and well-educated public requires information on scientific subjects for the fulfillment of personal interest and curiosity and for high school and undergraduate research. The development of the Science and Technology Park in downtown Skokie and the number of nearby academic institutions, hospitals, and pharmaceutical research firms translates to a number of Skokie residents employed in scientific and technical fields. Many fine university libraries are nearby and available to our patrons when they have exhausted our resources, therefore it is unnecessary to maintain depth much beyond the college level.

Selection Plan

Besides the standard selection tools, journals and popular periodicals such as *Science Books and Films* are checked for appropriate titles. Publisher's catalogs are also checked. Usually one copy of a title is ordered because these books can be expensive, but additional copies are ordered as needed. Hardcover editions are purchased when material is of lasting value while time-datable and ephemeral titles are purchased in paperback editions when available.

Retention and Weeding

Change is rapid in most scientific disciplines. Therefore materials more than three years old are checked for timeliness, and updated editions are acquired as needed. Philosophy and history of science are generally retained and new treatments added. Famous scientists' early works are kept for their historical value.

Development Plan

Worn copies are replaced if possible. Ephemeral material is withdrawn as it becomes obsolete. Esoteric and hypertechnical material is withdrawn, and books by well-credentialed scientists written for a general and intermediate audience are acquired. Textbooks are occasionally purchased to ensure complete coverage of a given subject.

	Past Collection Development Level	Current Collection Selection Level	Future Collection Development Level
500-Pure Sciences	3-	3	3
510-Mathematics	3	3	3
520-Astronomy	3	3	3
530-Physics	3	3	3
540-Chemistry	3	3	3
550-Sciences of Earths Other Worlds	3	2+	2+
560-Paleontology	2	3	3
570-Life Sciences	3	3	3
580-Botanical Sciences	3	2+	2+
590-Zoological Sciences	3	3	3

Subject: 600-Applied Science and Technology

Description

This section is probably the most diversified of the ten major divisions. The medical science area is the most heavily used, and it covers the history of medicine, nursing, anatomy, general health, diet and exercise, specific diseases, and individual fields of medicine such as geriatrics, pediatrics, obstetrics, psychiatry, etc. In the domestic science areas of the 630–640s, subjects cover cooking and nutrition, indoor and outdoor gardening, pets, child rearing, and sewing. A vast majority of these books are for the popular user. Another heavily used area is the 650s: management services. Most of the materials used are on the topics of job search, personal success in business, office skills and management, accounting, small business operation, management, advertising, and marketing. Materials range from popular to professional. The remaining areas cover engineering, building sciences, and chemical and industrial technologies. The majority of these books is on the subjects of automotive and electronic engineering and home building and repair and are used by hobbyists and do-it-yourselfers.

Influencing Factors

A large proportion of the population of Skokie own their own homes. As such, they are very interested in cookery, do-it-yourself projects, as well as personal and consumer health issues. Because many area residents are employed in areas of science and technology, books are on both a popular and professional level. Because of the expertise of the Skokie population, a higher development level is needed for the areas of manufacturing and building. These areas need to stay current with the changing technologies. Patrons have a strong interest in business subjects for career advancement. The Employment Resource Center draws users from Skokie and all surrounding communities who make heavy use of the employment and job search books.

Selection Plan

Besides the standard selection tools, publishers' catalogs and online resources are consulted. Individual auto repair manuals are purchased for most makes and models. Books with high interest and demand, especially résumé and health books, are purchased in multiple copies as demand indicates while other titles are purchased in single copies to give breadth to the collection. Inexpensive paperback editions are chosen over more expensive hardcover editions for materials that are time datable or of only current interest.

Retention and Weeding

The medical and business collections should be kept very current. Aside from classic titles, few books should be more than five years old; three years for medicine. Cookbooks should be weeded judiciously because of their potential historical value while pet books need to be kept so that all breeds are represented. Books in all other areas should be weeded in a three-year cycle for ephemeral, out-of-date, and infrequently used titles.

Development Plan

The 600 subject area is a very broad collection that has been developed fully to meet a diverse range of needs. The emphasis throughout the 600s is on keeping the area current and adding more popular materials, especially in the accounting and applied technology fields.

	Past Collection Development Level	Current Collection Selection Level	Future Collection Development Level
600-Technology	2+	2+	2+
610-Medical Sciences	3-	3-	3
620-Engineering and Allied Operations	2	2	2+
630-Agriculture and Related Technologies	2	2	2
640-Home Economics and Family Living	2+	3	3
650-Management and Auxiliary Services	3	3+	3+
660-Chemical and Related Technologies	2	2	2
670-Manufactures	2	2	2
680-Manufactures for Specific Users	2	2	2
690-Buildings	2	2	2

Subject: 700-The Arts

Description

The arts collection is made up of both popular and scholarly monographs in fine arts, music, dance, theater, film, sports, and games. The recreational and performing arts area of the collection, one of the most heavily used subjects, consists of books on motion pictures, television, theater, dance, games, and spectator and participatory sports. Another heavily used subject is the decorative and minor arts, which consist of books on handicrafts such as needlepoint, knitting, appliqué and quilting, jewelry making, and a broad spectrum of all types of crafts. Books of cartoons are also classified here. These books are geared to the beginning and continuing hobbyist. In the area of music, subjects include music appreciation, history and performance of music, musical scores, and opera libretti. These works cover classical and popular music from the introductory level to the general interest and initial study levels. The largest part of the collection consists of books on the history of art, works of noteworthy artists, architecture, sculpture, painting, drawing, photography, antiques, and decorative arts and furniture. These books range from popular to scholarly.

Influencing Factors

The high educational level and sophisticated interests of the community strongly influence the selection of materials for patrons' practical and recreational needs. Art exhibitions and musical events at the Art Institute, Museum of Contemporary Art, art galleries, Lyric Opera, Chicago Symphony, etc., influence patrons' interests and their demands for materials. The community's interest in sports as personal recreation and in Chicago sports teams is a major factor in purchasing all materials in this area. The many amateur theater and musical groups in the area come to the library for musical scores.

Selection Plan

Besides the standard selection sources and online resources, publishers' catalogs such as Rizzoli, Abrams, Aperture, Abbeville, Watson-Guptill, and university presses are checked for the subject of art. Music publishers' catalogs are also checked. Generally single copies of art and music books are ordered because of their cost. Opera libretti are ordered in multiple copies to meet patron demand during Lyric Opera season. Popular titles in sports may be purchased in multiple copies. Hardcover editions are preferred for all but the most ephemeral works.

Retention and Weeding

Weeding should be very judiciously done, removing only ephemeral works and damaged copies. New treatments which supersede earlier works will be added. Material on Chicago sports teams should be kept for historical purposes, but popular treatments of different sports should be kept current.

Development Plan

Emphasis is on developing the breadth of the collection rather than its depth. Essential or classic works should be replaced if lost or damaged whenever possible. The collection should be kept current to meet patrons' interests. This is especially important for the crafts and sports sections.

	Past Collection Development Level	Current Collection Selection Level	Future Collection Development Level
700-Arts	3	2+	3
710-Civic and Landscape Art	2	2	2
720-Architecture	2+	1+	2+
730-Sculpture	3	2	2+
740-Drawing, Decorative, Minor Arts	3	3	3
750-Painting	3	3	3
760-Graphic Arts	2+	2	2+
770-Photography	2+	2	2+
780-Music	2+	2+	2+
790-Recreational and Performing Arts	2+	3	3

Subject: 800-Literature

Description

The literature collection consists of style manuals and handbooks on English composition; books on preparing and delivering speeches; books on how to write letters, business and technical papers, and materials for publication. Collections of speeches, essays, and humorous writings as well as books of literary history and criticism comprise a major portion of the section. Anthologies of short stories, plays, and poems in both single-author volumes and anthologies complete the collection. Emphasis is on English and American literature, but classic and contemporary authors of note from many nations and cultures (particularly those represented in our community) are collected in translation. Because they are complementary collections, the 800s are shelved on the first floor near the fiction titles.

Influencing Factors

The library continues to maintain and augment the American and English literature subject specialty originally assigned to it by the North Suburban Library System Coordinated Acquisitions Program, now no longer in existence. Students at the high school and college level and local book club members make use of the books of American and English literary criticism.

Selection Plan

Besides the standard selection tools such as *Booklist*, *Library Journal*, *Choice*, *New York Times Book Review*, publishers' catalogs such as those of Twayne, Chelsea House, Samuel French, and those of universities and the small presses are used. Multiple copies are purchased of style manuals, contemporary drama, literary criticism of frequently studied authors, and classics of world literature. Usually one or two of those copies are purchased in hardcover; additional copies are purchased in paperback. One copy is usually sufficient for all other areas of the collection.

Retention and Weeding

Annually, American literary criticism and the plays of Shakespeare should be monitored because demand for these books is high and they frequently need to be replaced. American poetry and drama should be weeded in a two-year cycle to replace worn volumes and to withdraw ephemera. Other areas of the collection, being more stable, should be weeded in a three- to four-year cycle to replace damaged books and withdraw outdated material.

Development Plan

The literature collection is extensive. The emphasis is on preserving the depth of the collection. Toward that end, weeding should be done selectively and carefully. Copies of American literary criticism suitable for high school students need to be purchased regularly. Replacing and purchasing multiple copies of Shakespearean drama in single-play volumes is a continuing priority.

	Past Collection Development Level	Current Collection Selection Level	Future Collection Development Level
800-Literature	3-	3-	3-
810-American Literature	3+	3+	3+
820-English Literature	3+	3+	3+
830-Literature of Germanic Languages	3	3-	3-
840-Literature of Romance Languages	3	3-	3-
850-Italian, Romanian	3	3-	3-
860-Spanish and Portuguese Literature	3	3-	3-
870-Italic Literature Latin	3	3-	3-
880-Hellenic Literature Greek	3	3-	3-
890-Literatures of Other Languages	3	3	3
870-Italic Literature Latin	3	3-	3-
880-Hellenic Literature Greek	3	3-	3-
890-Literatures of Other Languages	3	3	3

Subject: 900-History and Travel

Description

The history collection is designed to include works of historical and contemporary interest, representing both scholarly and popular authors. The major emphasis is on United States history including books on Illinois, Chicago, and Skokie. A strong Holocaust collection features personal narratives, historical accounts, and scholarly works. There are numerous holdings covering all aspects of World War II. Collective biographies and works on geography and genealogy are also represented. The other major area of emphasis in the 900s is the current travel books collection. The latest editions of travel books and all of travel videos and DVDs are separately shelved and labeled to facilitate access to these very popular materials.

Influencing Factors

The library serves an educated and enlightened community that is comprised of diverse ethnic groups. Patron demand supports a collection of current and revised historical thought, opposing viewpoints, and major works that are considered classics. The age and affluence of the population create a demand for all types of travel materials. Skokie's Jewish population, which includes Holocaust survivors and their descendants, and the presence of the Illinois Holocaust Museum sustains a strong interest in materials on the Holocaust. The substantial number of World War II veterans in the community also contributes to the large number of requests for literature about that war. Similarly, a marked increase in the number of immigrants from Asia and Eastern Europe in recent years is influencing requests for more historical, descriptive, and travel resources relating to their homelands.

Selection Plan

For the majority of the 900s, publishers' catalogs are used on an as-needed basis to supplement the standard selection sources or to fill specific requests. Travel book selection requires more extensive use of publishers' catalogs and also relies on standing orders for annual travel series such as *Fodor's* and *Frommers*. Selection in this area strives to be responsive to newly published travel series, and ordering from journals should be supplemented with regular purchasing trips to local bookstores to keep current on new offerings. Multiple copies of a number of travel book titles are ordered in response to demand, and there is an ever-increasing number of instances where this would be appropriate, given available funds. In general, one copy of a historical work is ordered unless unusual demand is anticipated.

Retention and Weeding

Many works of history are timeless or classics and need to be retained; this is especially true for the original and reprinted Works Progress Administration (WPA) guides to the states that are in the library's collection. Careful selection and perception of future demand determine retention. Multiple copies of popular history are weeded as demand decreases. Within a three-year cycle, a complete examination of the area should be done. In the travel area, guide books are generally kept three years while travel memoirs are retained as long as there is interest in them. Multiple copies, books in poor condition, and superseded works are weeded on a continuing basis.

	Past Collection Development Level	Current Collection Selection Level	Future Collection Development Level
900-General Geography and History	2	2+	2+
910-Travel	2+	3	3
920-General Biography and Genealogy	2	2+	3
930-History of Ancient World	2	2+	2+
940-History of Europe	3-	3-	3
Holocaust World War II	3	3	3
950-History of Asia	2	2+	2+
960-History of Africa	2	2	2
970-History of North America	2+	3-	3
980-History of South America	2	2	2
990-History of Other Areas	2	2	2

Development Plan

Given the population shifts that have occurred in Skokie in recent years, the major emphasis of selection in the 900s will be to support the traditional and longstanding areas of interest described above while being responsive to the interests of a growing population of well-educated Asians and Eastern Europeans. Additional materials may need to be added to the 950s to support increased interest in Asia and the Middle East. Attention will also have to be given to developing an even-handed representation of the various viewpoints surrounding ongoing, worldwide ethnic conflicts. Selection of travel books will continue to reflect the present emphasis of making the collection attractive to an even wider range of users through inclusion of more varied types of travel materials to a wider range of locales. There will also be a continuing effort to provide more extensive coverage of Eastern Europe and Asia.

Subject: Biography

Description

The biography collection consists of factual materials about people from all walks of life and all nationalities from ancient times to the present. Autobiographies, memoirs, and volumes of correspondence are also included in the collection.

Influencing Factors

A well-informed community has a strong interest in reading about the lives of influential and interesting people. The materials are used by those pursuing independent study and by casual browsers. High school and college students from Skokie and the surrounding communities use the biography collection for their assignments.

Selection Plan

Standard selection tools including *Kirkus*, *Library Journal*, *Booklist*, and online resources are used regularly. Publishers' catalogs are occasionally consulted. One to three copies of a title are ordered depending on patron demand. Hardcover editions are preferred over paperbacks.

Retention and Weeding

Retention of titles is based on the biographee having enduring importance. Popular works about people of current interest are withdrawn as soon as interest has ceased. Weeding of extra copies, books in poor condition, and ephemeral works must be done yearly. Within a three-year cycle a complete reexamination of materials that are infrequently used must be done to maintain space for new books.

Development Plan

Works need to be purchased to keep up with popular demand and to maintain a well-balanced and wide-ranging section. Replacement of worn-out or missing titles is ongoing.

	Past Collection Development Level	Current Collection Selection Level	Future Collection Development Level
Biography	3+	3	3

Subject: Reference

Description

The adult reference collection contains materials covering all subjects and ranges in degree of difficulty from high school level to beginning research level. Most subject areas include practical and popular as well as scholarly materials. The aim is to provide current information on all subjects and historical information in areas of continuing interest.

Electronic resources play a major role in the reference work in the twenty-first century. The library's subscription databases and e-book collections along with a command of Internet resources and Web search engines provide the reference librarian instant access to the full content of resources unfathomable to librarians of the pre–Internet era.

Books purchased for the reference collection now tend to be those easily accessible for ready reference as well as specialized codes and directories not readily available online. There are a number of areas in reference that receive special emphasis. An extensive collection of business resources serves business professionals, the small businessman, individual investors, and job seekers.

The Employment Resource Center includes an abundance of career directories, small business handbooks, preparation books, specialized national and local job-listing publications, and a variety of career encyclopedias and guides.

A longstanding emphasis on English and American literature in the nonfiction collection is supported in the literature reference section by biographical materials, and compilations of criticism. This collection is supplemented by several databases including *Novelist, Granger's World of Poetry,* and *Literature Resource Center.*

Materials on Skokie, Chicago, and Illinois are located throughout the reference collection. The Skokie Obituary File (1962–present) and Newspaper Index (1983–present) are digitized and are available on the Internet. Other local information is being compiled digitally as part of the library's Digital Past Project. Cataloged Skokie materials include municipal documents (budget, ordinances, planning documents, school, park district, library publications, etc.), descriptive publications, photographs, and some historical resources.

Illinois and Chicago materials are primarily descriptive and historical, although publications of government agencies that have general interest and long-term applicability are included. This is not a rare book collection but one that acknowledges the public's strong interest in local topics and the difficulty of easily obtaining such information.

A depository collection of contemporary documents issued by Illinois state government agencies is housed in Skokie's reference area and available for circulation. This resource makes Skokie's acquisition of some state publications unnecessary.

Influencing Factors

Skokie is a community whose residents consistently look to the information resources of the library to meet needs occurring throughout their life. Nowhere is this more evident than in reference. Whether the information sought is related to child rearing, academic assignments, employment, business, professional development, consumer concerns, or recreational and leisure pursuits, there is a high expectation on the part of the Skokie public that the library will either have the answer or know where to find it. Residents now expect to have access to authoritative information sources through electronic databases anytime and anywhere.

The origins of the library's sophisticated, well-informed, and demanding patrons can be traced to several of the village's primary characteristics. Skokie has long been known for its strong emphasis on education, both formal and self-directed, for children and adults. Presently there is a continuation of this emphasis among immigrant residents. Many of these individuals stress the academic achievement of their children, seek to further their own professional skills, and look to the library for assistance.

Associated with the community emphasis on education are a variety of formal educational institutions: elementary schools whose students have increasingly sophisticated information needs, two high schools that serve the entire township, a branch of a community college with an active adult education program, and National-Louis University. A large number of residents are enrolled at colleges and universities in the Chicago area. The library does not attempt to cater to specific course requirements of students; nevertheless, all of these ingredients influence the nature of the library's clientele and shape the perceptions and expectations they have of their local library.

	Past Collection Development Level	Current Collection Selection Level	Future Collection Development Level
Reference Book Collection	3+	3	3
Ref. Electronic Collection	3	3+	3+

SUBJECT: Reference

Skokie's location in a major metropolitan area affects the reference service. The number and variety of academic institutions, special library collections, and commercial establishments create sophisticated demands on Skokie's reference service and collection.

Selection Plan

Selection of reference materials is based on subject coverage, timeliness, affordability, and usefulness. Reviews and recommendations of materials are consulted before purchasing reference materials. *Library Journal, Booklist*, and *Choice* provide the most thorough and objective reviews of new reference materials. Other bibliographic resources are consulted when needed. Reference materials are periodically examined in person at conference exhibits and bookstores.

Ads and brochures are checked for new titles because of their timeliness. Appropriate, regularly published titles are placed on standing order to ensure prompt receipt of the most current edition. Normally, only one copy of a standard reference book is purchased. If the contents and format make it appropriate for the circulating collection, however, additional copies are ordered. Among print items, both hardcover and paperback titles are selected.

An increasing number of reference materials are being acquired in nonprint formats. In some cases, both print and nonprint versions of a title are available. Decisions on format are the responsibility of the coordinator of Information Services, who takes into consideration the usage of the material by patrons and librarians. Online versions of reference titles are purchased only if the expansion of the functionality of the product is significant enough to offset the cost differential of the reference source.

Other factors influencing the choice of an electronic resource include its ease of use, relevance of content, dependability of access, and timeliness of the information available. The use of databases needs to be continually monitored and selections re-evaluated on the basis of usage reports.

Reference titles published periodically may be placed on standing order. Price, frequency of publication, overlap with other titles, or specialization sometimes make standing orders impractical. Some alternatives to standing orders are considered such as ordering every two or three years or deciding to order a new edition on a case-by-case basis. The entire standing order list is to be reviewed at least once a year.

All selectors should inform the coordinator of or assistant coordinator of Information Services of new editions and important new reference materials within their respective subject areas.

Recommendations by patrons of new reference materials or the identification of areas of collection weakness are given immediate consideration.

Selection of reference materials for Adult Services and Youth Services is coordinated so that no unnecessary duplication will occur and so that the content of each reference resource is appropriate to the needs and educational level of its user. Youth Services and Adults Services reference selectors consult each other regarding selection of reference materials that may be appropriate to both departments.

Retention and Weeding

Retention decisions are based on the likelihood of significant continuing historical interest in a field or title. Older titles in constantly changing areas such as the sciences are less likely to be retained. Weeding is done on a continuous basis to make room for newer titles. Skokie, Illinois, and Chicago publications are generally retained because of their uniqueness and patrons' need for local historical information. Availability of reference materials in electronic formats affects retention and weeding practices. In the current market, the continuing availability of archival information through electronic means is by no means assured, therefore restraint will be exercised in determining when older book and index materials should be weeded. For materials that are only kept in current editions, electronic resources may offer a good alternative and would then not be retained in paper copy.

Development Plan

The availability of an increasing variety of electronic resources in all forms provides many new opportunities for access to information. The library's reference resources must include those technological resources that increase and improve access to information.

In general, development will be guided by the fact that the reference service continues to be utilized by local residents. The reference print collection will decrease in size. Expansion of reference will be in access to electronic resources.

Subject: Periodicals

Description

Periodicals are available in a variety of formats: print, microform, and full text through online resources. Over 898 titles are available in print and microform. The library subscribes to many databases that contain full-text periodical articles allowing users the option of reading them online, printing them on paper, e-mailing them, or downloading them.

Influencing Factors

The library acquires and maintains a periodical collection to serve the informational, educational, and recreational needs of the community. Patrons' demands for current information are more often now met by the resources found in electronic databases. As a result, the collection has diminished in size and is now more focused on recreational reading. The needs of the community's diverse ethnic populations are addressed by the inclusion of foreign-language titles. Space considerations and availability of a variety of full-text electronic resources influence journal selection and retention.

Selection Plan

The library's objective is to maintain a well-balanced general periodical collection of current titles in a broad range of subject areas. Patron and staff suggestions for purchase are evaluated by the Periodicals Committee through consulting various selection tools. Reviews of new titles are read on a regular basis. Availability of titles in electronic format is considered.

Criteria used in format decisions:

1. Does the electronic version significantly enhance access to the information?
2. If electronic format is provided, is the paper or microfilm version needed for current backup or retrospective archiving?
3. Is the electronic, print, or microfilm version cost effective for amount of anticipated patron use?
4. Does the electronic version include full text and full images? Are both in demand?
5. Issues of cost, equipment, frequency of updates, licensing arrangements, number of simultaneous users supported, speed of access, and ease of use.

Retention and Weeding

Because of space considerations, the size of the bound periodicals collection must be limited. Retention is influenced by a title's use and availability by electronic means. Print titles that the library receives in microform will not be bound.

Development Plan

The print periodical collection, while quite extensive, is limited by physical space restrictions and by the increase in periodicals in electronic format. Most print titles are kept for a fixed number of years rather than as indefinitely archived runs. With the advent of increased access to full-text and full-image articles, the need for the breadth of print subscription titles, especially of academic and specialized journals, will decrease. The focus of the print collection should be to serve patrons' popular interests with a representative core of academic journals. The primary area for development in access to periodicals will continue to be in the area of electronic access. Microform subscriptions will be maintained for archival coverage of core periodicals. By increasing electronic access to periodicals, the library can approach supporting the research in depth by electronically superseding the physical limitations of storage space.

	Past Collection Development Level	Current Collection Selection Level	Future Collection Development Level
Popular Periodicals	2+	3+	3+
Scholarly Periodicals	3	2+	2
Business Periodicals	2+	3+	3+

Subject: Federal Documents

Description

For many years the library, although not a depository, has included a substantial number of Federal publications in virtually all areas of its collection. The library's ongoing philosophy has been one of actively seeking to acquire, catalog, and interfile any Federal publications that support our general collection development policy and to give them the same accessibility as other materials in the collection.

There has been no attempt to develop Federal publications as a document collection per se, but rather to select those publications that, regardless of format, contribute to the content of their subject area and patron interest the way any other material would.

Federal publications appear frequently in the reference collection, are cataloged as circulating nonfiction in almost all areas of reading interest, and are represented in the periodical collection by such titles as the *Monthly Labor Review* and *FDA Consumer*. The library's catalog offers links to the online counterparts of many of our print government publications as well as to electronic-only titles and notable government Web resources.

Federal publications are selected for general and, occasionally, advanced interest levels. Beginning research-level bibliographies, indexes, and directories have been acquired where needed to provide orientation to specialized topics and to facilitate appropriate referral to other institutions and resources.

Influencing Factors

Federal publications are important because they give the general public unique access to what their government is doing and how it is doing it, thereby contributing to the development of an informed citizenry. Furthermore, the Federal government is a prolific publisher encompassing practically all areas of knowledge, much of which is of little interest to commercial publishers but contains an abundance of useful, sought-after information. Also, information published by the Federal government is frequently requested and well received because the source is regarded as authoritative.

Another significant influence on the library's acquisition of Federal publications is the existence in the Chicago metropolitan area of so many excellent university and special collections—both in documents and in general library materials. The proximity of Skokie to these library resources has made it unnecessary to select many of the specialized titles and series that the Federal government publishes or to retain selected titles for long periods. The Federal depository libraries continue to be of importance to us because of the expertise of their staff, the depth of their collections, and their ability to offer our patrons free access to online, fee-based government resources.

The rapid changes that have occurred in recent years in format, printing, distribution, and accessibility of Federal publications also influence our collection. Foremost among these changes are the transition for a majority of Federal publications from a print to an electronic format with distribution on the Internet, the widespread and immediate access to Federal government information to anyone with Internet access that this dissemination enables, and a trend toward decentralization as individual Federal government agencies increasingly originate and distribute their own information electronically and in doing so bypass some of the traditional coordinating functions of the U.S. Government Printing Office (GPO).

Selection Plan

Federal publications, regardless of format, are selected by following the guidelines for selection and development established for the appropriate subject area. But specialized or technical publications intended for advanced interest or beginning research–level users may be acquired when there is interest in a topic and little is published on the subject by commercial publishers, when the Federal government viewpoint on a particular topic is of interest to the public, or when a topic becomes the focus of much public scrutiny and thus warrants acquisition of more specialized materials than normal.

Increased decentralization in the printing, distribution, and announcement of Federal publications has resulted in a more fragmented acquisitions process for nondepository libraries, and it has become one that relies almost entirely on online resources.

The primary source for ordering Federal publications sold by the (GPO) is its online U.S. Government Bookstore. The Catalog of U.S. Government Publications (CGP), which is the online counterpart of the *Monthly Catalog of Government Publications*, supplements the bookstore and serves as a national resource for identifying electronic and print titles published by all branches of the Federal government.

Announcements of new print and electronic titles are searched for in the bookstore's weekly listings of major releases, the CGP's "New (Electronic) Titles" feature, the "What's New Archive" on GPO Access, and Bernan's *Government Publication News*. The GOVDOC-L discussion list offers timely access to a broad spectrum of practical, procedural, and policy issues concerning Federal publications. *Census Product Update* and the weekly *GPO Congressional Publication Releases* are also reviewed for coverage in those areas.

E-mail requests are sent directly to individual Federal agencies to obtain publications not sold by the GPO or, in some instances, a free copy of a for-sale item. In-demand

SUBJECT: Federal Documents

serials and annuals are acquired through standing orders with the GPO and Bernan, a commercial firm.

Selection of Federal publications also includes ordering bulk quantities of certain free, widely requested publications and forms for public distribution, such as the IRS and FAFSA forms.

Retention and Weeding

With the exception of the special situations outlined under "Selection Plan," retention and weeding of Federal publications follow the policies established for the subject area in which they are located. Continuing public interest and availability online or at area depositories are considered.

Development Plan

Retrospective ordering of Federal publications occurs only when the government publishes appropriate materials in areas designated as needing further development by other selectors. But the possibility of this is limited by the rapidity with which titles become out-of-print, cease publication, or are issued only electronically.

The library's role is gradually changing from one of selecting tangible items for the collection to one of facilitating the public's access to online Federal publications and resources. This reflects changes in the format, public accessibility, and location of numerous publications but not a change in philosophy about the inclusion and integration of Federal publications into our collection and into the services we offer the public.

Development of the collection will occur by our cataloging the online versions of Federal publications when we own the earlier print editions; linking in our catalog to notable Federal websites and to electronic-only titles that we formerly would have considered appropriate for purchase; featuring Federal online resources on the library's Online Information Resources website; and directly assisting the public in locating the Federal information it seeks.

Subject: Illinois Documents Depository Collection

Description

One of the major functions of the Illinois Documents Section of the Illinois State Library is to provide access for all Illinois citizens to comprehensive collections of the publications of Illinois state government agencies. It does this by acquiring the publications issued by these agencies, regardless of their format, and (when sufficient copies are available) distributing them through a cooperative statewide network of 24 libraries designated as Illinois Documents Depository Libraries. The Skokie Public Library and Northwestern University Library are the two libraries in the NSLS that house Illinois Documents Depository collections.

Traditionally, the publications making up the collection have included any document, report, directory, bibliography, rule, regulation, newsletter, pamphlet, brochure, periodical, or other printed material paid for by funds appropriated by the General Assembly or issued at the request of a state agency. With the growth of the Web and an increase in electronic publications, new regulations have been added requiring state agencies to submit either the URL or the electronic version of any such publications to the Illinois State Library. The Illinois State Library then takes responsibility for making these records available online.

The diversity of topics presented in the Illinois Documents Depository Collection mirrors that of the general library collection but with a unique Illinois emphasis and perspective that is invaluable to its citizens. Virtually any functions, programs, or activities of any state agency that find their way into one of its print or electronic publications are likely candidates for our Illinois Documents Depository shelves or online catalog. Publications in our collection encompass legislative and regulatory information; state finances and economy; social, health and welfare needs; consumer issues; education; taxation; business; labor; agriculture; and natural history.

The collection is separately shelved on ranges adjacent to the reference collection and is organized into three distinct sections: monographs and serials, which are arranged by Dewey number; annual reports, which are arranged by issuing agency or title; and periodicals, which are arranged by title. Most of the titles in the collection are permitted to circulate.

All of the items are catalogued, as required by Illinois Documents Depository regulations. Cataloging is central to the integration of the documents into the rest of the collection and is critical for public access. It enables the library to fulfill its depository responsibilities of providing both access and reference assistance to all Illinois citizens and of responding to interlibrary loan requests. The library's catalog provides links to the online counterparts of many of our print Illinois state publications, as well as to electronic-only titles and notable Illinois government websites.

Influencing Factors

Since the 1970s, an Illinois Documents Depository Collection has been housed at the library. The collection was administered by staff of the NSLS until 1992, when the system terminated its depository status. At that time the library, recognizing the importance of these materials to Skokie and NSLS member libraries, applied for and was granted depository status.

Selection Plan

The State Library's Illinois Documents Section obtains and distributes (free of charge) Illinois state government publications to each depository library, and this determines, for the most part, the contents of the collection. Complementing the traditional distribution process for print publications is the recently inaugurated Illinois Electronic Documents Initiative (EDI), a Web-accessible electronic depository that offers permanent public access to official publications of the state that have been issued in electronic form. On a practical level, EDI will facilitate the loading of cataloging records for these electronic documents into our catalog.

The monthly *Illinois Documents List* is scanned for publications that may be of interest to the library but that have not been distributed through the depository library network. In some cases, the general popularity of a publication or its usefulness for reference warrants our ordering additional copies for Skokie's collection directly from the issuing agency. Bulk quantities of certain free popular Illinois state government forms and publications such as *Rules of the Road* and *Handbook of Illinois Government* are ordered for public distribution.

Retention and Weeding

The Illinois State Library retains ownership of the documents in the depository. The depository is required to keep most items for a minimum of seven years after which a list of withdrawn documents must be submitted to the State Library. The State Library, in turn, offers them to other depository libraries for their selection. Presently the library retains most documents for a seven to ten-year period, relying on such factors as continuing importance, interest in the subject, unique character of the material, and space to determine retention.

Development Plan

Since the structure and content of this collection is governed by external laws and regulations, development is likely to take the following directions: continuing the process of linking in our catalog to the online versions of print publications and adding new records for electronic-only documents; featuring notable Illinois state government online resources on the library's *Online Information Resources* website; and directly assisting the public in locating Illinois state government information.

Subject: Fiction

Description

Classic literature, popular bestsellers, and general fiction from all time periods and from all parts of the world make up the fiction collection. The fiction collection represents one of the oldest traditions of humankind, that of storytelling. Fiction not only entertains, but enriches human understanding by presenting and describing life's experiences in an imaginative rather than factual manner. The emphasis in the collection is on American and English authors, but representative authors from all other countries are also included in English translations. While current bestsellers are bought in multiple copies, works of first authors, short-story writers, and small-press writers are also purchased. A collection of bestsellers, the Most Wanted Collection, is shelved with the new book section.

Influencing Factors

A community that reads all types of fiction and expects newly released books immediately is the strongest factor in determining selection and the number of copies ordered. In addition to high school students, there are numerous community college, university, and returning older students who use the library's collection for assignments. Numerous adult book discussion groups throughout Skokie and the north suburban area, and adult book classes at the local universities and colleges create demand for critically acclaimed writers, classic authors, and foreign authors. A large, ethnically diverse community has interest in works by Jewish, Israeli, Indian, Russian, Korean, Polish, and Chinese authors. Increasingly these authors are being requested in English translation as well as in the original language. Local and state writers are also purchased and retained in the collection.

Selection Plan

In addition to the standard selection tools and online resources, reviewing sources such as the *New York Times Book Review*, various genre-related discussion lists on the Internet, and printed genre bibliographies are looked at regularly. Publishers' catalogs, small-press catalogs, and ads are also used, especially to find first novels, reprints of classics, and foreign novels. Annual editions of *Fiction Catalog* and *What Do I Read Next* are used to check that we have purchased key titles. Out-of-print book sources are searched for replacement of missing and out-of-print novels.

The Most Wanted collection of books consists of best-sellers, primarily fiction, but does include the occasional nonfiction title of current interest. These titles are nonreservable. Multiple copies up to forty each are purchased to meet current demand, to save wear and tear on permanent copies, and to keep numbers of reserves down to manageable figures. The number of copies per title is at the discretion of the selector, who uses his or her expertise to predict demand for a particular author or title. We purchase one copy per five reserves of high-demand titles. The Most Wanted books are usually less than a year old, unless in high demand because of a newsworthy event or a movie tie-in.

Reviewing tools for these are the same as other fiction titles and include *Booklist*, *Kirkus*, *Publisher's Week*, *Library Journal*, and the *Chicago Tribune* and *New York Times Book Review Sections*. One to three copies of other titles are purchased, depending on demand. When multiple copies are needed for older titles, paperbacks are often purchased, but it is important to have a combination of both hardcover and paperback copies for popular titles. Special emphasis is given to collecting the complete works of important and popular authors, as well as filling in series titles.

Retention and Weeding

Weeding in the fiction area must take into account the cyclical nature of author popularity. Sources such as *Fiction Catalog* and other genre and subject bibliographies like *Genreflecting* may be consulted before a title is withdrawn. In addition, inclusion on online readers' advisory tools such as *NoveList* will be taken into consideration for retention of a title. Generally, one or two copies of a title will be retained. Literary classics, regional authors, and well-recognized contemporary authors are retained, often in multiple copies as fits demand. Weeding of additional copies of books in poor condition and of ephemeral authors must be done yearly. Within a three-year cycle a complete reexamination of materials that are infrequently used must be done to maintain space for new books.

	Past Collection Development Level	Current Collection Selection Level	Future Collection Development Level
Classic American and English Works	3	3	3
Foreign Fiction in translation	2+	2+	3
General Fiction	3	3	3
Most Wanted	3+	4	4

Development Plan

Since the collection is quite extensive, very little retrospective development is needed. But the emphasis should be on replacing worn-out editions of older but important titles with new hardbound editions or new paperbacks to encourage patron use. As older authors in English and American literature are reprinted, these books should be purchased. A list of high–demand, out-of-print hardbound books is kept and used-book sources are periodically checked. The focus in the fiction collection should be on purchasing as broadly and as widely as possible to give the collection depth while having enough multiple copies of high-demand books to satisfy patron requests as quickly as possible. More e-books will be made available on our library's website if usage demands.

Subject: Mystery

Description

The mystery section includes detective and mystery writers since the time of Edgar Allan Poe and from all parts of the world. Espionage writers whose works have an emphasis on mystery rather than adventure are cataloged in mystery rather than in fiction. Romantic suspense authors are generally cataloged in fiction unless their work has more of a mystery theme than a romance theme. The collection is very extensive and tries to have the complete works of important and popular authors as well as subgenres, e.g., police procedurals, hard-boiled detectives, English cozies, and so on. Reprints of older authors, either in hardcover or paperback, are an important part of the collection. The mystery anthologies—808.8372—are shelved after the mysteries to encourage patron browsing.

Influencing Factors

The mystery genre is one of the most popular subjects in the library and has a high circulation. Patrons read all older authors in addition to reading more recent authors. Most mystery addicts want to read all the works of their favorite authors and each volume of a series, so it is important to have complete sets.

Selection Plan

Supplementing the standard selection tools, reviewing sources such as the *New York Times Book Review* and Internet discussion lists such as Dorothy L are looked at regularly. Publishers' catalogs and ads such as those from Mysterious Press and St. Martin's Press are checked for both new books and reissues of older titles. One or two copies of each title are generally ordered unless an author is extremely popular and more copies are needed. Special emphasis is given to collecting the complete works of important and popular authors as well as all titles in high-demand series. Copies of titles from our published bibliographies and bookmarks should be collected and retained. Original mystery paperbacks and reissues of older titles available only in paperback are also included in the mystery collection.

Retention and Weeding

Weeding in the mystery area is very difficult because older authors are still very popular. Generally one copy of a title will be kept of all but the most ephemeral books. Because of space considerations, weeding of extra copies and of books in poor condition must be done yearly. Within a three-year cycle a complete reexamination of materials that are infrequently used is done to maintain space for new books.

Development Plan

As older titles are reissued they should be purchased, and worn-out editions of popular titles should be replaced with either new hardbound or new paperback editions to encourage patron use. Purchasing should be broad to bring as many new authors and new subgenres as possible into the collection.

	Past Collection Development Level	Current Collection Selection Level	Future Collection Development Level
Mysteries	3+	3+	3+

Subject: Romance

Description
The romance section includes a variety of subgenres: contemporary romance, time-travel romance, and historical romance, to name a few. The collection tries to have representative works by important and popular authors. The romance anthologies—808.83—are all shelved at the end of the romance books to encourage browsing.

Influencing Factors
Romance is a popular genre and readers often find an author and are interested in reading every book this author has written. While some romances are ephemeral and are published only in paperback, others have become classics of the field and should be retained.

Selection Plan
Supplementing the standard selection tools, reviewing sources such as the *Romantic Times* and Internet discussion lists are looked at regularly. Publishers' catalogs and ads are checked for both new books and reissues of older titles. One or two copies of each title are generally ordered unless an author is extremely popular and more copies are needed. Copies of titles from our published bibliographies and bookmarks should be collected and retained. Original romance paperbacks are also included in the romance collection.

Retention and Weeding
Weeding in the romance area can be very difficult because older authors are still very popular. Generally one copy of a title will be kept of all but the most ephemeral books. Because of space considerations, weeding of extra copies and of books in poor condition must be done yearly. Within a three-year cycle a complete reexamination of materials that are infrequently used is done to maintain space for new books.

Development Plan
Worn-out editions of popular titles should be replaced with either new hardbound or new paperback editions to encourage patron use. Purchasing should be broad to bring as many new authors as possible into the collection.

	Past Collection Development Level	Current Collection Selection Level	Future Collection Development Level
Romance	3	3	3

Subject: Science Fiction

Description

The science fiction section includes science fiction and fantasy writers from all parts of the world and from classic to contemporary authors. Most fantasy has been cataloged with science fiction instead of with fiction. The science fiction classification now covers such genre types as high and low fantasy, gothic fantasy, science fantasy, sword and sorcery novels, "hard" science fiction, alien being, alternate worlds, vampires, robots, and space travel and time travel novels. Futuristic novels, speculative fiction and World War III–type novels by major writers such as Margaret Atwood and Doris Lessing are usually put in fiction. Paperbacks of new and reissued authors are an important part of the collection. The science fiction anthologies—808.8376—are all shelved at the end of the science fiction books to encourage browsing.

Influencing Factors

Science fiction continues to be popular with young adults but adult readers are presently the largest user group. Because science fiction fans are loyal series readers, special attention must be given to maintaining complete series, most often with paperback reprints of earlier volumes. Recent trends toward more authors being published in hardcover format has contributed to the stability of the collection.

Selection Plan

In addition to the standard selection tools, *Locus* is the best single reviewing medium. It has strong, in-depth reviews and alerts the selector to books being published in Britain, which appear in later editions in the United States. Publishers' ads and catalogs are also followed regularly to keep up with new titles and new authors.

Retention and Weeding

Weeding in the science fiction area is very difficult because older authors are still read. One copy of a title will be kept of all but the most ephemeral books. Sources such as *Fiction Catalog* and specialized science fiction reference sources may be consulted before a title is withdrawn. Weeding of extra copies and books in poor condition must be done yearly. Within a three-year cycle complete reexamination of materials that are infrequently used must be done to maintain space for new books.

Development Plan

The emphasis is on bringing in a range of new authors, buying reprints of classic authors, filling in series titles by popular authors, and replacing titles that are in poor condition.

	Past Collection Development Level	Current Collection Selection Level	Future Collection Development Level
Fantasy	2-	2-	2
Science Fiction	2	2	2

Subject: Western

Description

The western section is small, but has a core of dedicated readers. The genre is separated from general fiction to highlight it for readers that might otherwise have trouble finding their favorite kind of novel. Many of the titles are available only in paperback.

Influencing Factors

While not hugely popular in Skokie, the library strives to maintain a core collection with additional popular titles of a more ephemeral nature.

Selection Plan

Usually, only one copy of a title will be purchased. General fiction selection tools and online sources will be used. Original paperbacks are included in this section.

Retention and Weeding

Generally one copy of a title will be kept of all but the most ephemeral books. Because of space considerations, weeding of extra copies and of books in poor condition must be done yearly. Within a three-year cycle a complete reexamination of materials that are infrequently used is done to maintain space for new books.

Development Plan

As older titles are reissued they should be purchased, and worn-out editions of popular titles should be replaced with either new hardbound or new paperback editions to encourage patron use.

	Past Collection Development Level	Current Collection Selection Level	Future Collection Development Level
Western	2	2	2

Subject: Adult Graphic Novels

Description

The graphic novels in this collection are more adult in theme than those found in the Teen Corner, either in subject matter, visual content, or both. Here, the visual representation of the story is just as important as the written words, if not more so. While these books are called graphic novels, in fact some of them are actually nonfiction or biography.

Influencing Factors

Books are purchased to appeal to an adult audience. Storylines should reflect an older reader; titles intended for a younger audience would be purchased for the Teen Corner collection.

Selection Plan

The standard selection tools and online resources are used to determine choices. Publishers' catalogs are also used. Single copies are purchased unless demand dictates otherwise. Titles are chosen on the basis of their graphic representation as well as their written story.

Retention and Weeding

All titles will be retained unless in poor physical condition. Weeding on the basis of circulation and lasting value should only be done if space becomes limited.

Development Plan

This is still a new and growing collection. It is expected to increase in size fairly quickly because the medium is very popular.

	Past Collection Development Level	Current Collection Selection Level	Future Collection Development Level
Adult Graphic Novels	0	2	2

Subject: Teen Corner

Description

The young adult collection is an area called the Teen Corner. It comprises both fiction and nonfiction books selected specifically to meet the recreational and informational needs of teenagers. The fiction section consists largely of young adult novels; genre literature covering mystery, science fiction, fantasy, and romance; and adult novels and bestsellers that are popular with teenagers. Nonfiction books reflect topics of current interest and popularity and cover a wide range of subjects including music, sports, biography, humor, teen social adjustment, health, and etiquette. There is also a section with graphic novels including manga.

Influencing Factors

Books for school assignments and research papers are generally not included in this collection except those that are on topics that relate directly to teenagers such as anorexia nervosa and teen suicide. Fiction that has been assigned is sometimes purchased in multiple copies to meet demand. While the high school libraries emphasize curriculum-related materials, the Teen Corner highlights recreational and informational books for teens.

Selection Plan

The standard selection tools and online resources especially useful for this area include *Booklist, Library Journal, School Library Journal, Kirkus Children and Young Adult Reviews,* and *Kliatt*. Publishers' catalogs are also used. Since books in paperback format are preferred by teen readers, titles should be ordered in this format whenever possible. Multiple copies are purchased as needed.

Retention and Weeding

Generally, only titles that continue to be popular are retained. Other titles are weeded and replaced by new materials of current need and interest. Sources such as Young Adult Library Services Association's annual lists of *Best Books for Young Adults* and Betty Carter's *Best Books for Young Adults* may be consulted before a title is withdrawn.

Development Plan

Retrospective development in the young adult collection is not necessary because of the changing nature of the literature in response to the needs of young adults.

	Past Collection Development Level	Current Collection Selection Level	Future Collection Development Level
Teen Corner	2	3	3

Subject: World Language

Description

The world language collection consists of books in Arabic, Chinese, French, German, Greek, Gujarati, Hebrew, Hindi, Hungarian, Italian, Japanese, Korean, Malayalam, Polish, Russian, Spanish, Urdu, Vietnamese, and Yiddish. The Chinese, Hebrew, Korean, Polish, Russian, and Spanish collections are rather extensive and include classics, theater, poetry, and selected nonfiction and fiction titles. The library has a representative sampling of titles in French, German, Greek, Hungarian, and Italian.

Influencing Factors

The library acquires and maintains a world language book collection to serve the recreational and informational needs of its diverse community. Growing Asian and Russian populations have prompted the building of the collection in these languages. Materials in Hebrew and Yiddish are purchased to serve the interests of the Jewish community. Materials in Gujarati, Hindi, and Urdu are being purchased to meet patron demand.

Selection Plan

Publishers' catalogs, websites, and bookstores are used to select current titles. Consideration is given to patron requests. Emphasis is given to fiction, biography, and titles of current interest for adults. Standing orders from OCLC are used for Hindi, Urdu, and Gujarati publications and are sometimes used to supplement other languages as well.

Retention and Weeding

The world language collection is weeded regularly. Materials with low circulation, in poor condition or obsolete are weeded.

Development Plan

Emphasis will be placed on acquiring current fiction, biography, and how-to books in Chinese, Gujarati, Hindi, Korean, Polish, Russian, Spanish, and Urdu. Other language materials will be considered for purchase as demand indicates.

	Past Collection Development Level	Current Collection Selection Level	Future Collection Development Level
French, German, Italian	2	1	1
Chinese, Gujarati, Hindi, Korean, Polish, Spanish, Urdu	1	2+	2+
Russian	1+	3+	3
All other languages	1	1	1

Subject: Literacy/English as a Second Language Collection

Description

Materials for adults who are functionally illiterate and for those who are learning English as a second language (ESL) are shelved in a separate area. Graded language exercise books, citizenship books, and audiovisual materials comprise the area. The materials appear in the online catalog with the ESL designation and a Dewey Decimal call number.

Influencing Factors

The library is a member of the Oakton District Public Library Literacy Coalition, and ESL classes are held in the library every week.

Selection Plan

Literacy/ESL materials are rarely reviewed. Selection choices are made using online resources and by looking through publishers' catalogs.

Retention and Weeding

All materials are kept until they are in poor condition.

Development Plan

The library maintains and follows the Oakton District Public Library Literacy Coalition guidelines for the collection. This area will increase to include more audiovisual materials and software.

	Past Collection Development Level	Current Collection Selection Level	Future Collection Development Level
Literacy	1-	2	2

Subject: Large Type Books

Description

The large type book collection duplicates many titles already in the library in standard type. Classic literature, popular fiction, and genre fiction (including mystery, romance, adventure, and western titles) make up the fiction collection. The majority of nonfiction books consist of titles that are popular in standard format.

Influencing Factors

Skokie has a number of residents for whom large type books are an important library resource. The Skokie Accessible Library Services (SALS) program was launched with Federal grants to help provide materials for people with disabilities. The funds augmented the large type book collection, and the library is committed to maintaining it for all users.

Selection Plan

Selection is made from traditional large type publishers. Major publishers such as Random House are now publishing a select group of large type popular titles simultaneously with the regular type editions. Large type publishers are publishing a select group of popular titles in softcover, which seem to circulate as well as the hardcovers.

Retention and Weeding

Since large type books are seldom available once the initial print run is exhausted, the utmost care must be taken not to discard valuable titles that cannot be replaced. Books in poor condition are discarded first. Titles in good condition but no longer circulating are also discarded.

Development Plan

Because large type books are seldom reprinted, emphasis should be on purchasing the most desirable titles soon after publication, with double copies of those that are likely to remain popular in the future. New works need to be purchased to keep up with popular demand and to maintain a well-balanced and wide-ranging section.

	Past Collection Development Level	Current Collection Selection Level	Future Collection Development Level
Large Type Fiction	2	3	3
Large Type Nonfiction	1	2+	2+

Subject: Paperbacks

Description

This collection is intended for adults who prefer reading popular fiction, genre fiction, and classics in mass market and trade paperback formats. Set up as a browsing collection (including mysteries, romances, standard fiction, science fiction, bestsellers, and classics) it has become an integral part of the popular materials collection.

Influencing Factors

Factors that influence the selection of paperbacks are the reading and format preference of our patrons. Heaviest circulation seems to be in fiction, especially the romances and mystery genres. It is important to maintain a wide variety of fiction and genre titles to satisfy demand for current as well as retrospective titles. Because the large size of the library's fiction collections, the separately displayed paperback collection facilitates browsing.

Selection Plan

Most of the materials purchased are selected from Baker and Taylor's *Paperclips*. When demand is predictable, two copies or more of each title are purchased. Some series are purchased, particularly in romance and science fiction. Occasionally donations of paperbacks are selectively culled for popular titles in like-new condition.

Retention and Weeding

Paperbacks are retained only as long as they are in good condition and circulating. Weeding is done on the basis of physical condition. To keep the collection fresh and current, it should be weeded on a monthly basis. Withdrawn titles from popular series or authors are replaced whenever possible.

Development Plan

The collection should be kept current and attractive.

	Past Collection Development Level	Current Collection Selection Level	Future Collection Development Level
Paperbacks	2-	2	2

Subject: Music CDs

Description

The music collection includes popular mainstream genres, show tunes, and classical music of all types. It is currently predominantly on CD. This general collection is 35% classical and 65% popular.

Influencing Factors

Our population is a varied one and has diverse tastes. Skokie patrons demand top-quality recordings and the latest technical advancements. Demand dictates a strong collection of current popular mainstream and classical recordings. Skokie has a large Lyric Opera Guild chapter and members demand a strong opera collection. Circulation statistics will influence purchasing patterns for the collection. Trends in the recording industry influence availability of formats and their prices. Circulation of genres has been variously effected by the popularity of downloading music.

Selection Plan

Besides the standard selection tools, reviewing sources such as *Billboard* are checked regularly. Publisher and vendor catalogs (*Midwest Tapes, AEC One Stop*), specialty catalogs, as well as online sources for music are consulted. Classics and contemporary works in all genres are represented. Multiple copies are purchased if warranted by demand.

Retention and Weeding

Weeding should be continuous and based upon circulation records. Materials in poor or damaged condition are evaluated and either removed from circulation, repaired, or replaced as necessary.

Development Plan

The goal is to maintain a broadly representative collection rather than a comprehensive, in-depth collection of music. Each genre will be reviewed on a rotating basis to be certain important works, composers, or performers are not missing. Changing technology in the audio field may affect format composition.

	Past Collection Development Level	Current Collection Selection Level	Future Collection Development Level
Classical Music CD	2	2	2
Popular Music CD	2	3	3

Subject: DVDs

Description

The DVD collection consists of feature films including the nonreservable Hot Pix DVDs as well as educational, how-to, performance, travel, and documentary films. The collection also includes a significant number of world language films, some subtitled and some not; anime films and television shows; and a group of television dramas and comedies. The collection is 70% feature films and 30% nonfiction and television.

Influencing Factors

DVDs are extremely popular with the patrons. The library acquires and makes available DVDs to serve the general informational, educational, and recreational needs of the community. Classics as well as currently popular films are collected. Because budgetary and space constraints, the library will purchase multiple copies of only the most popular feature films. In addition, films that exhibit appropriateness and expected use and value to the collection through the long term are acquired. The multiethnic nature of the community dictates a generous selection of world language films, especially Russian, Chinese, and Hindi. Television dramas and series are purchased only if they are award-winning, very popular, or have valuable special features. No attempt is made to collect every episode of an entire television series. Patron requests for specific DVDs will be considered and purchased if the film is appropriate to the collection. Circulation statistics influence purchasing patterns for this collection. Changing technology in the DVD marketplace is a factor to be considered in the long-range development of the collection.

Selection Plan

Reviewing sources such as *Billboard* and newspaper reviews are looked at regularly. Publishers' catalogs, distributors' catalogs (*Midwest Tapes*, *Instructional Video*, *Facets*, *Film Movement*) and ads are also used to identify current high-interest releases, nonfiction films, and replacements. Various DVD guides are referred to for retrospective selection. Multiple copies are ordered only for high-interest feature films.

Retention and Weeding

DVDs with little or no circulation and multiple copies of former high-interest features are considered for weeding. Replacement copies for missing, worn, and damaged DVDs are ordered only if the quality (appropriateness, expected use, and value to the collection through the long term) of the item warrants it.

Development Plan

A balance (through new titles, replacements, and weeding) will be maintained between the two broad DVD categories (features and nonfiction). DVDs of old classic and well-reviewed films will be purchased as they become available. Effort will be made to increase the number of world language films, and nonfiction DVDs of all kinds will be purchased to replace and augment the video collection. The DVD collection size will grow at a significant rate as the video collection declines. The effect of emerging technologies could supplement or replace DVDs in the future.

	Past Collection Development Level	Current Collection Selection Level	Future Collection Development Level
Feature Films	2	3	3+
Nonfiction Films	2	2	2+

Subject: Spoken Word

Description

The spoken word collection includes prose (fiction and nonfiction, classics and current popular titles); poetry, plays, radio, and television transcriptions; speeches; and instructional recordings. The latter includes world language instruction, business management, and motivational and self-help recordings. This general collection is 45% fiction; the balance is nonfiction and other categories. Downloadable e-audiobooks are also purchased.

Influencing Factors

The users of this collection are varied and have diverse tastes. Circulation statistics influence purchasing patterns for the spoken word collection. Trends in the recording industry influence availability of formats and their prices.

Selection Plan

Besides the standard selection tools, reviewing sources are checked regularly. Publisher and vendor catalogs (*Recorded Books*, *Books on Tape*, *Brilliance*, *BBC Audiobooks*, *Tantor*, *Teaching Company*) as well as specialty catalogs are consulted. Classics and contemporary fiction and nonfiction works are represented. Unabridged versions are preferred. Self-help materials (primarily business and psychology) are selected on the basis of quality and reputation of the provider.

Retention and Wedding:

Weeding should be continuous and based upon circulation records. Materials in poor or damaged condition are evaluated and either removed from circulation, repaired, or replaced as necessary.

Development Plan

The goal is to maintain a broadly representative collection rather than a comprehensive, in-depth collection of spoken word recordings. Nonfiction spoken word titles of subjects suitable to this medium should be selected in as broad a range as possible to provide access for patrons who, for whatever reason, prefer to listen rather than to read. Changing technology in the audio industry may affect the format composition of the collection in the future.

	Past Collection Development Level	Current Collection Selection Level	Future Collection Development Level
Spoken Word	2	3	3

Subject: CD-ROMs

Description
The CD-ROM collection includes informational, educational, and "edutainment" products.

Influencing Factors
Changing technology in the CD-ROM and computer industries will be an important factor in the development of the collection.

Selection Plan
The standard selection tools and online resources reviewing sources are looked at regularly. Publisher and vendor catalogs are also used to identify available titles.

Retention and Weeding
The CD-ROM collection is a shrinking collection. CD-ROMs with little or no circulation will be considered for weeding. CD-ROMs in poor or damaged condition will be evaluated and either removed from circulation, repaired, or replaced as necessary.

Development Plan
Patron requests for specific CD-ROM titles will be considered and purchased if the program is appropriate to the collection. The dominance of online databases and websites has made this format decline significantly in popularity.

	Past Collection Development Level	Current Collection Selection Level	Future Collection Development Level
CD-ROMs	0	2	1

Subject: Teen Video Games

Description

The video games are predominately entertainment oriented and are meant for teens over the age of 14. Games of current interest will be purchased with a rating of T for Teen. Games with a rating of E for Everyone or Everyone 10+ will be purchased for Youth Video Games. Platforms will be added or dropped on the basis of popularity.

Influencing Factors

Games appear in a variety of media: popular movies tie-ins, TV show tie-ins, and book tie-ins, as well as sports themes, so all will be considered for purchase.

Selection Plan

Websites such as GameSpot and retailers that sell games can be used to identify and evaluate popular games.

Retention and Weeding

Games will be kept as long as they are still in good condition and are up-to-date enough to be played on current platforms. Games will not be withdrawn as soon as a platform is upgraded but will be retained as long as they are being played.

Development Plan

This will be a growing collection, but no attempt will be made to buy to demand. The collection size is limited by the amount of space for storage and the high security that is needed to protect them.

	Past Collection Development Level	Current Collection Selection Level	Future Collection Development Level
Teen Video Games	0	1+	2

Subject: Digital Books, Audiobooks, and Videos

Description
The library provides access to a collection of downloadable books, audiobooks, and videos through the online catalog and the library website. Some these materials are shared with the North Suburban Digital Consortium, and some are provided only to the library.

Influencing Factors
As MP3 players improve and computer access speeds up, these materials are more and more in demand.

Selection Plan
The same criteria used in selecting books, audiobooks, and videos are used for selecting digital materials in those same areas. Those materials whose content is more in demand or of lasting value may be purchased in numerous formats including print, CD, DVD, and downloadable.

Retention and Weeding
Since the materials are online and take up no physical space, there is no need for weeding. Access to some materials may be withdrawn if usage drops.

Development Plan
As new sources for downloadable materials become available, they will be evaluated for content, ease of use, and applicability to the collection. It is anticipated that this collection will continue to expand.

	Past Collection Development Level	Current Collection Selection Level	Future Collection Development Level
Digital Materials	0	1+	2

G. Youth Services Department

The Youth Services Department occupies 15,966 square feet on the east side of the first floor. Glass exhibit cases provide a welcoming entrance, along with a 125 gallon fish tank. The "Ask Here" desk is situated in the center, and its low height encourages even the youngest children to interact with a librarian. Books are displayed on a number of display units to promote the best nonfiction, fiction, and picture books. Four study rooms provide a quiet place to study for young people, and homework computers in this area allows student access to word processing and research databases including Live Homework Help, a highly used service. An inviting craft room allows for creative play and family interaction, with craft kits available at the Youth Services Desk. A program room complete with twinkling stars is the perfect site for programs for babies, toddlers, and preschoolers.

A parent–teacher area serves the needs of both parents and teachers. The "Come On In" area, with a special needs computer and a bookcase of special needs materials, is featured in the front of the department to provide a prominent welcome to families who have children with special needs for learning.

School textbooks, located behind the Youth Services Desk, are provided for use in the library. Voice of Youth Advocates (VOYA) bookcases promote this special reading program with multiple copies of VOYA books for students in third through eighth grade. The fiction and easy fiction collection provides colorful bibliographies and books on the end panels. Quotes from Illinois authors help to inspire and connect children to the creative process.

A large nonfiction collection provides information resources for young people up through eighth grade. A large banner based on Paul Zelinsky's *Rumpelstiltskin* hangs above the folk and fairytale section. Another banner that promotes the department's theme, "Read, Imagine, Explore," hangs on the wall just inside the front entrance—Wendell Minor's "Cat, What is That?" This theme seeks to inspire children to write, draw, and paint, since the artists of these books live or grew up in Illinois just like them.

A large preschool area invites families with young children to come in and spend some time at the library. Preschool computers, the Peek-a-Book listening station, a puppet stage, other toys that encourage imagination, and a wonderful collection of board books, picture books, and readers create a great place to explore and learn.

A computer lab offers children who are eight through junior high access to the Internet. This attractive room consists of twelve individual stations and one lab assistant station. The lab assistant is scheduled for all of the lab's open hours. The Junior High Zone provides a listening station, teen magazines and paperback series, and another place for students to work together or alone.

The department has added popular video games, graphic novels, puppet books, and reader nonfiction collections in recent years. The world language collection is strategically located on a busy aisle and is popular with our families from other countries.

The Youth Services Department is committed to offering the best quality of materials, programs, and services to meet the ever-changing needs of our population.

Description of Youth Services Collection
by Classification

Subject: Picture Books

Description

Picture books may be either educational or recreational in intent. They are distinguished by their illustrations, which serve to either supplement, extend, or, in the case of wordless books, supplant the text. In most instances, picture books are read aloud to the child or the child studies the pictures and creates his or her own text.

Books for independent reading are in the reader section. Concept books, i.e., books that develop a child's understanding of colors, shapes, etc., fall into the picture book category, as do mood books, which create a feeling for a time, place, or experience. Often picture books are designed to help a child develop coping skills, understand peer and family relationships, or develop a positive self image. Board books for toddlers, stressing colorful, simple objects, are shelved separately as a browsing collection. ABC/123 books, which focus on the learning of ABCs and numbers, are also shelved as a separate collection.

Influencing Factors

Diversity in the ethnic makeup of the community creates a demand for books depicting a variety of cultures. Families with a single parent or mixed ethnic background stimulate a need for books depicting similar family units. Common bibliotherapy themes, such as moving, starting school, birth of a sibling, etc., are often requested, as are concept books to meet the beginning educational needs of preschoolers. Books appearing on school reading lists are in great demand as are books related to popular TV programs.

Selection Plan

Besides the standard selection tools, publishers' ads, catalogs, and BWI are consulted. Bibliographies such as *A to Zoo: Subject Access to Children's Picture Books* may be consulted if the collection is lacking titles in a specific high-demand area. Titles by authors of proven popularity would automatically be collected in multiples, but generally, because of limited shelving, initial orders would be for no more than two copies. An exception would be if the title is extremely well reviewed and is thought to have vast general appeal, particularly to our biggest user group: preschoolers and their parents. Spinoffs from popular movies and TV programs would be strongly considered if they were educationally reputable.

Children's classics, such as Beatrix Potter books, will be retained and updated as new editions become available. Pop-up books are rarely purchased because of a shortened shelf life, but flap books, such as the Eric Hill Spot books, are still purchased routinely. Books with specially reinforced bindings are purchased for titles that require a longer shelf life.

Retention and Weeding

Books are usually kept in the collection as long as their physical condition and continued circulation warrants. Single copies might be weeded from the collection if circulation statistics indicate no appeal; multiple copies of a title will be kept only if circulation is sufficient. An exception might be if the title appears in important bibliographies.

Development Plan

The collection is well-developed and most of the important titles and authors are represented. Worn and damaged copies of popular titles will be replaced depending on the availability of the book. The continuing emphasis will be on developing a well-balanced collection that will meet the diverse interests and needs of our community. This is a stable area.

	Past Collection Development Level	Current Collection Selection Level	Future Collection Development Level
Picture Books	3-	3	3

Subject: Readers

Description

This collection specifically addresses the reading-development needs of preschoolers through second graders. It ranges from prereaders, (stressing phonics, word groups, and vocabulary building) to beginning chapter books. Many of the books are publishers' series targeted for a specific reading level. In many cases vocabulary is controlled, text is well spaced, and margins are wide. Illustrations are usually secondary to text. Nonfiction readers are also included here but are shelved separately from fiction titles. Three different reading levels are differentiated by stickers and are shelved separately.

Influencing Factors

Some series appear on school lists and are in high demand. Parents request books that teach prereading skills to preschoolers and also those that supplement the reading texts of an elementary school child. Children usually seek books at reading levels that are comfortable; series with a continuing cast of characters tend to be popular.

Selection Plan

Besides the standard selection tools and online sources, ads and catalogs from publishers are consulted. Emphasis is placed on finding a wide variety of books at varied reading levels. Multiple copies are the norm, particularly if the author or series is popular. Paperbacks are not purchased if there is a hardbound alternative. Some series are on standing order.

Retention and Weeding

Books are kept as long as they continue to circulate and are in good condition. Popular but worn titles are replaced if possible. Multiple copies are checked for condition and circulation on an annual basis because shelving in this area is limited. The collection is thoroughly analyzed and weeded in a three-year cycle.

Development Plan

Though this collection circulates extremely well, no more real growth can be realized. Instead the collection should be closely monitored for usage patterns. Additional titles and series should be purchased accordingly.

	Past Collection Development Level	Current Collection Selection Level	Future Collection Development Level
Readers	1+	2+	2+
Nonfiction Readers	0	1+	2+

Description

The easy fiction collection is designed to meet the needs of the child with a second through fourth grade reading level, now ready to make the transition to shorter chapter books or picture books with a longer text and more mature theme. These books tend to have a younger protagonist, simpler themes, and require less maturity than a J Fiction book; plot development tends toward the episodic, reducing the need for a long attention span.

Influencing Factors

Attention should be given to the needs of the very young reader who has a higher reading ability than maturity level. Themes of books should be appropriate to his maturity level. School demands for students to read from recommended lists and subject areas should be considered. The cultural diversity of Skokie should be reflected in the collection, creating a need for books reflecting a variety of cultures.

Selection Plan

Besides the standard selection tools and online resources, reviews as well as publishers' ads and best-books lists are consulted. Books by popular authors such as Beverly Cleary or books that are part of popular series such as the American Girls Collection are bought in multiples. Titles in popular series are usually bought in their entirety, with less-well-reviewed titles represented by single copies until demand warrants additional copies.

Retention and Weeding

Titles are kept only as long as they are in good condition and continue to circulate. Titles are replaced and supplemented as needed. Books in poorer condition are usually retained only if of proven popularity and replacement. Demand for titles is the determining factor as to how many copies are retained. A single copy of a title of low popularity might be retained if the book appears in awards lists or bibliographies. Weeding should be done on an annual basis with an in-depth perusal of titles in a three-year cycle.

Development Plan

Series with favorable reviews will be purchased in their entirety then studied for literary merit and popularity. Worn copies of popular titles will be replaced with new editions or copies.

	Past Collection Development Level	Current Collection Selection Level	Future Collection Development Level
Easy Fiction	1+	2+	2+

Subject: J Fiction

Description

The J[QY: spell out?] fiction collection is made up of titles to meet the recreational needs of students with a fourth through sixth grade reading level. The needs of gifted students, low-ability students, and the needs of students from diverse cultures are taken into consideration. Recognized children's classics are often represented in a variety of editions, both hardbound and paperback. An effort is made to include all books that have won children's literary awards. Genres including sports, animals, science fiction, fantasy, adventure, ghost stories, historical fiction, and mystery are all represented and are identified by stickers. Short-story collections written by a single author are also included in this section.

Influencing Factors

School demands for students to read from recommended lists and subject areas are taken into consideration; these titles are represented by at least one copy. The ethnic diversity in the community demands a supply of books representing many cultures. A long-established Jewish community has demonstrated a desire to have prominent Jewish and Israeli authors represented. For pleasure reading an attempt is also made to purchase all books written by popular authors and all books in series that have gained wide acceptance by a selected readership.

Selection Plan

The standard selection tools and online sources are used as a source for titles for the older readers. Reviews as well as publishers' ads and best-books lists are consulted. Publisher's catalogs are read in an effort to identify early upcoming titles of popular authors. Books by popular authors are bought initially in multiple copies.

Retention and Weeding

Titles are kept as long as they continue to circulate and are in good condition. Titles are replaced and supplemented as needed. Books in poorer condition are retained if of proven popularity and replacement, even in paperback format, is not possible. Demand for a title is the determining factor in how many copies are retained. Weeding should be done on an ongoing basis with an in-depth perusal of titles in a three-year cycle.

Development Plan

The library will continue to collect books that meet the diverse recreational needs of its patrons. A concerted effort will be made to replace classic and worn but popular titles with new editions or copies, both hardbound and paperback. This collection is a stable collection.

	Past Collection Development Level	Current Collection Selection Level	Future Collection Development Level
J Fiction	3-	2+	3

Subject: Junior High Fiction

Description

The junior high fiction collection is made up of titles to meet the recreational needs of students with a sixth through eighth grade reading level. The needs of gifted students, low-ability students, and students from diverse cultures are taken into consideration. Recognized children's classics are often represented in a variety of editions, both hardbound and paperback. An effort is made to include all books that have won children's and young adult literary awards. Genres such as sports, animal, science fiction, fantasy, mystery, realistic fiction, and historical fiction are all represented. Short-story collections written by a single author are also included in this section.

Influencing Factors

School demands for students to read from recommended lists and subject areas are taking into consideration; these titles are represented by at least one copy, and in many cases multiple copies. Whenever possible, this demand is met by supplying additional paperback copies. A greater ethnic diversity in the community is creating a demand to supply books that are multicultural in nature. A long-established Jewish community has demonstrated a desire to have prominent Jewish and Israeli authors represented. For pleasure reading an attempt is also made to purchase all books written by popular authors.

Selection Plan

Besides the standard selection journals, we have popular series on standing order. Reviews as well as publisher's ads and best-books lists are consulted. Publisher's catalogs and jobber catalogs are read on a regular basis in an effort to identify early upcoming titles by popular authors. Books by popular authors are bought initially in multiple copies.

Retention and Weeding

Titles are kept as long as they continue to circulate and are in good condition. Titles are replaced and supplemented as needed. Books in poorer condition are retained if of proven popularity and replacement is not possible. Demand for a title is the determining factor in how many copies are retained. A single title will usually be retained if the book appears in a standard bibliographic tool such as *Best Books for Children*. Weeding should be done on an ongoing basis with an in-depth perusal of titles in a three-year cycle.

Development Plan

The library will continue to collect books that meet the diverse recreational needs of its patrons. A concerted effort will be made to have a well-rounded, multicultural collection. Every effort will be made to replace classic and worn but popular titles with new editions or copies, both hardbound and paperback. This collection is a stable collection.

	Past Collection Development Level	Current Collection Selection Level	Future Collection Development Level
Junior High Fiction	2	2+	3

Subject: Youth Graphic Novels

Description

These are stories told in graphic form, usually in sequential boxes of art with dialogue and narrative. Art is the primary means through which the story is told in a graphic novel. Graphic novels usually focus on the adventures of one character or set of characters and are often produced in series. In fact many established literary series have now been published in graphic novel format. Nancy Drew and The Hardy Boys are prime examples. The youth graphic novels collection consists of graphic novels in which story and character are simple and straightforward, and content is age appropriate (no violence, sexuality, etc.). But artwork can be of very high quality even at this level. The youth graphic novels collection focuses on independent readers from grades 2–5. Each title in a graphic novel series circulates as a single unit.

Influencing Factors

The collection is used by children. It is an extremely popular format and circulates very well. The goal of the selector is to help our patrons feel that this is their own collection. Their input is encouraged.

Selection Plan

Selection criteria include patron requests, age suitability, and ongoing titles in popular series. Collection development resources and an online discussion list are used to stay abreast of new titles that may be of interest to our kids.

Retention and Weeding

The youth graphic novels collections are in the development stage. The collections tend to weed themselves, since all titles are purchased in paperback and circulate so heavily that eventually they must be withdrawn. The collection is at present small enough that the selector is able to periodically check circulation stats for every title. Popular titles are replaced as they are withdrawn. If a title is not circulating, it will not be replaced.

Development Plan

Both junior high and youth graphic novels collections are still in the development stage. The demand for youth and junior high graphic novels is so strong that the list of titles to be purchased far exceeds the budget currently allotted for the two collections. The plan is to continue adding to both collections from this list while also replacing worn-out but popular titles as funds will allow.

	Past Collection Development Level	Current Collection Selection Level	Future Collection Development Level
J Graphic Novels	0	1	2
Junior High Graphic Novels	0	1	2

Subject: Youth Series Paperbacks

Description
Popular series constitute the primary focus of the collection. The turnover rate is high. Paperbacks meant for older readers are designated as junior high paperbacks and are shelved separately.

Influencing Factors
The paperback format is very popular with young people. The most popular series and authors are carefully monitored, and titles are shelved in a browsing format.

Selection Plan
Besides the standard selection tools, Title Source 3 from Baker and Taylor is used regularly. Replacement copies are ordered for books weeded because of condition. Series titles with high circulation are automatically replaced. A paperback series standing order is used to reduce the staff time involved in tracking paperback series. This has also enabled us to be more current in providing titles in regularly issued series.

Retention and Weeding:
Weeding should be done every six months to remove items in poor condition. Items that circulate infrequently should be weeded regularly.

Development Plan
The collection should be maintained as a popular collection with a high circulation rate. This is an area that will remain stable in size.

	Past Collection Development Level	Current Collection Selection Level	Future Collection Development Level
Youth Series Paperbacks	2	2+	2+
Junior High Series Paperbacks	2	2+	2+

Subject: Easy Nonfiction

Description

The easy nonfiction collection consists of materials to meet the recreational, informational, and educational needs of younger children. The materials are highly pictorial and therefore valuable to a wide age range of library users. For this reason easy nonfiction is shelved with the J nonfiction collection even though it is considered to be a separate collection. The collection is particularly strong in fairy tales, animals, biographies, holidays, and ecological concerns.

Influencing Factors

This is a heavily used collection. Young children have a natural curiosity about many topics. Topics such as poetry, animals, astronomy, and dinosaurs are popular for pleasure reading. Students also use the library to complete assignments. Fairy tales, science projects, biographies, and ecological concerns are recurring assignments.

Selection Plan

Besides the standard selection tools, Title Source 3 from Baker and Taylor is checked regularly. Journal reviews are occasionally used. Multiple copies are purchased in subject areas that are heavily used. Replacement copies of worn materials are ordered if the information is still current.

Retention and Weeding

The collection is weeded to remove out-of-date materials. Science, technology, geography, and social issues in particular are examined carefully because of the rapid change in these areas. Worn materials are weeded on an ongoing basis.

Development Plan

A very modest growth can be expected.

	Past Collection Development Level	Current Collection Selection Level	Future Collection Development Level
Easy Nonfiction	2-	3-	3-

Subject: Nonfiction

Description

The nonfiction collection consists of materials to meet the informational, educational, and recreational reading needs of school-age children. Though the collection is developed for balance with all subject areas represented, community interest and demand plus the availability of materials on a topic create some areas of greater strength. The areas listed below are the collection's areas of strength. Because reading levels vary from child to child, all areas try to include material with higher and lower reading levels.

000s: Circulating encyclopedias, titles about computers, and unexplained phenomena such as UFOs.

100s: Psychology, astrology, ghosts, and personal growth and development.

200s: Religions of many cultures and mythology.

300s: Folk and fairy tales, disabilities, holidays, civil rights, the Constitution, and environmental issues.

400s: Language and language instruction, particularly English and sign language.

500s: Science projects, astronomy, dinosaurs, earth sciences, and life sciences.

600s: Human body, health sciences, pets, cooking, transportation, space flight, and inventions.

700s: Crafts, hobbies, music, sports, cartoons, motion pictures, creative arts, and art history.

800s: Poetry, plays, short story anthologies, classics, and some criticism.

900s: United States history, world history, particularly the World Wars, Native Americans, ancient civilizations, states, foreign countries, collective biographies, and contemporary and historical biographies.

Influencing Factors

Although the schools all have library media centers, students frequently use the public library to complete their assignments. Teachers also use the collection not only for lesson planning but to supply additional classroom resources for enrichment and as resource materials for students' reports. Some topics such as science projects, states, countries, astronomy, ancient cultures, the human body, biographies, and environmental issues are recurring assignments with heavy seasonal use. These high-demand areas are developed both in depth and breadth. Children consistently use the collection for recreational reading in such diverse areas as sports, magic, pets, cartoons, drawing techniques, and crafts.

Selection Plan

Besides the standard selection tools and online sources, Title Source 3 from Baker and Taylor is checked regularly. Multiple copies are occasionally purchased in subject areas that are heavily used. Replacement copies of worn materials are ordered if the information is still current.

Retention and Weeding

Within a period of two years the collection is weeded to remove out-of-date materials. Science, technology, geography, and social issues in particular are examined carefully because of the rapid change in these areas. Worn or damaged materials are removed on an ongoing basis.

Development Plan

This is an area of some growth.

	Past Collection Development Level	Current Collection Selection Level	Future Collection Development Level
J 000s (Generalities)	2	2	1
J 100s (Philosophy)	1	2-	2-
J 200s (Religion)	1	1+	2-
J 300s (Social Sciences)	2	2+	2+
J 400s (Language)	1	1+	2
J 500s (Pure Sciences)	2	2+	3-
J 600s (Technology)	2	2+	3-
J 700s (Arts)	2+	2+	2+
J 800s (Literature)	3	2	2
J 900s (Geography and History)	2	2+	3-
J Biography	2	2	3-

Subject: Parent/Teacher Collection

Description

Though some of these titles may be duplicated in Adult Services, Youth Services maintains a collection drawing together those books offering practical suggestions and ideas for rearing, entertaining, and educating children from infancy through grade eight.

Emphasis will be given to the following areas:

1. Books offering help with parental concerns such as child development, discipline, sibling rivalry, learning disabilities, etc.
2. Books suggesting strategies for improving reading competency in children as well as suggesting titles for family and individual reading.
3. Books offering suggestions for sources of information and help, e.g., yellow pages for parents.
4. Books offering suggestions for entertaining young children such as quiet entertainments, crafts, and family outings.
5. Books dealing with the educational needs of young children from the dual perspectives of parent and daycare provider/teacher.
6. Homeschool resources for at-home educators.

Influencing Factors

Top priority will be given to the concerns of new parents dealing with the day-to-day challenges of raising children of varying ability. The special needs of parents acting as scout leaders, school volunteers, and so on will be considered as well as the needs of elementary school teachers, preschool teachers, and daycare providers. Also considered will be the special needs of an ethnically diverse community in which parents are coping with the demands of raising children in a new culture.

Selection Plan

Besides the standard selection tools, ads and publishers' catalogs will be consulted. Newspapers, parenting magazines, and trade and educational bookstores are a source of additional titles.

Retention and Weeding

Titles will be retained as long as the material is recent enough to be reliable and the condition and circulation of the book warrants its inclusion. Titles will be checked annually for condition and circulation; every two years the collection will be critically examined and weeded.

Development Plan

Since the collection serves parents, daycare providers, and teachers, special attention should be taken to see that the needs of all are addressed and that a proper balance of material is achieved. Titles offering practical rather than theoretical help are desirable. Patron suggestions are encouraged. This collection is heavily used and should continue to reflect current trends in both child rearing and education.

	Past Collection Development Level	Current Collection Selection Level	Future Collection Development Level
Parent/Teacher Collection	2-	3	3

Subject: Reference

Description

The Youth Services reference collection is a collection of materials supporting the reference needs of children through eighth grade. Professional materials for librarians, teachers, and parents are also included, especially in the area of children's literature. Some titles duplicate those in the Adult Services reference collection.

Influencing Factors

The reference collection includes material to satisfy a child's personal interests and curiosity about the world as well as the students' need for information for school assignments. Online databases provide extensive information on many subjects and are accessible both in the library and often from home. Support materials are provided for professional staff as well as school librarians, educators, and parents.

Selection Plan

Publishers' catalogs as well as general selection tools are used to develop this collection. Juvenile reference books sometimes duplicate books contained in the circulating collection or in the Adult Services reference collection. Popular reference sources are on standing order.

Retention and Weeding

A useful reference collection must be current. Weeding should be done annually to remove outdated items. Encyclopedias are added to the circulating collection after they are withdrawn from reference.

Development Plan

Reference books will be replaced by current editions as they become available. Electronic sources such as databases and encyclopedias will replace print sources as they become available.

	Past Collection Development Level	Current Collection Selection Level	Future Collection Development Level
Reference	2+	3	3
Electronic Resources	1	2+	3-

Subject: Periodicals

Description

The Youth Services periodical collection contains more than 50 titles. Materials to support the recreational, informational, and educational needs of children through eighth grade are included as well as materials for parents, teachers, daycare providers, and librarians. A selection of comic books is also purchased for circulation.

Influencing Factors

One consideration should be the needs of children to obtain materials that not only reflect current trends and fashions but also reflect a variety of ages and abilities. Another consideration should be the needs of teachers and parents. Teachers need new curriculum information, particularly preschool teachers who do not have the support of a school library. Parents need information on raising their children in a rapidly changing world.

Selection Plan

New periodicals and sample issues are evaluated by the Periodicals Committee.

Retention and Weeding

Back issues of popular magazines are generally kept for one year. Magazines that are likely to be used for school assignments and parenting, and professional magazines are kept as space permits.

Development Plan

Electronic format is preferred for periodicals that support school assignments. The periodical collection should be expanded to include popular titles that are devoted to specific, high-interest subjects not adequately covered in the book collection.

	Past Collection Development Level	Current Collection Selection Level	Future Collection Development Level
Periodicals	2-	2	2+

Subject: World Languages

Description

This collection includes books and nonprint materials for children in preschool through eighth grade in eighteen different languages. The collection responds to the needs of non-native speakers of English, students of foreign languages and their teachers, and children with a general interest. Translation of English materials as well as materials originally written in the foreign language are included. Books with texts in both English and another language are available and are popular with parents and grandparents who are not yet comfortable with English alone.

Influencing Factors

Immigrants are well represented in Skokie's population. Many come from Russia, Korea, China, India, Mexico, and the Philippines, creating a demand for children's materials in these languages.

Selection Plan

Purchase of a variety of titles rather than multiple copies is preferred.

Retention and Weeding

Weeding is done annually on the basis of the physical condition of each item and on the current need for materials.

Development Plan

Russian, Hindi, and Gujarati are emphasized in response to the changing makeup of the community. More Spanish language materials will be purchased.

Foreign Language	Past Collection Development Level	Current Collection Selection Level	Future Collection Development Level
Chinese, Korean	1	2	2-
Russian, Spanish, Urdu	1+	2-	2
French, German, Greek, Italian, Japanese	2	1	1
Hebrew	0	2	2-
Hindi, Gujarati, Tagalog	0	1-	2-
Other Languages	1	1	1

Subject: Large Type and Braille Books

Description
The large type collection is made up of popular and classical fiction as well as nonfiction. The collection is intended to meet the educational and recreational needs of children from third to eighth grade who may have visual or reading disabilities, although it is not limited to this group. The large type collection duplicates materials already in the library in standard type. The braille collection was largely funded by a grant from Land's End, but will continue to be maintained by the library.

Influencing Factors
Children read large type books for classroom assignments and individualized reading. The Skokie Accessible Library Services (SALS) program was launched with Federal grants to help provide materials for people with disabilities.

Selection Plan
Large type books are ordered from publishers' catalogs.

Retention and Weeding
The collection is weeded annually. Books that are outdated or in poor condition are discarded.

Development Plan
Attention will be paid to purchasing the most popular titles as soon as they are available in large type. Also, older oversized large type editions will be replaced with more current formats as budget permits.

	Past Collection Development Level	Current Collection Selection Level	Future Collection Development Level
Large Type	2-	2-	1
Braille	1	1	1

Subject: Music CDs

Description

The CD collection contains the music of most of the popular entertainers for children. Materials are selected for children through age 14. The materials selected for children through age eight receive the higher circulation.

Influencing Factors

Skokie is a culturally diverse community with a demand for multicultural materials. The needs of educators and parents are also considered. Popular appeal is considered; therefore Disney recordings and book tie-ins are usually purchased. Downloadable music has not yet had a big effect on the selection and number of CDs purchased for children.

Selection Plan

Selection is done from catalogs such as *AEC Onestop*. Recommended lists are also used. Demand requires that multiple copies of most titles be purchased, especially those popular with preschoolers and their parents.

Retention and Weeding

Worn or damaged materials are weeded from the collection, as are materials with low circulation.

Development Plan

This popular collection demands constant collection development. New release titles and titles topping the children's music charts should be purchased. Titles reflecting diverse cultures should be added as they become available, as should materials that would be particularly helpful to parents and educators. High-circulation titles that are worn should be replaced by new copies. A higher percent of the budget should be spent on music for preschoolers and their parents because of the need for heavy duplication of these popular titles. Changing technology in the audio field may affect format composition.

	Past Collection Development Level	Current Collection Selection Level	Future Collection Development Level
Music CDs	2	3	3
Junior High Music CDs	2	2	2

Subject: Spoken Word

Description

The spoken word collection includes prose fiction, non-fiction, and poetry. The predominant format is CD, and audiocassettes are no longer being purchased. The collection is predominantly popular fiction with the balance being nonfiction and poetry in diverse areas. Most titles are Junior High or J fiction with some additional titles in easy fiction, readers, and picture books. In addition, picture book titles are ordered in book and CD combinations that are shelved together in hanging bags.

Influencing Factors

A large and continually growing number of young patrons and their families use the spoken word collection both in their automobiles and in personal CD players. Popular titles and school curriculum needs influence purchasing patterns for audiobooks. Family listening titles predominate.

Selection Plan

Besides the standard selection journals, we have CD spoken word standing order plans from Listening Library and Recorded Books, both of which feature the newest available selections in popular children's recorded books. Publisher catalogs are consulted as well. Unabridged versions are preferred.

Retention and Weeding

Audiobooks are kept as long as they continue to circulate and are in good condition. Audiocassette format materials are not replaced unless titles are now available in CD format. When worn or damaged, popular titles are replaced if possible. The collection is analyzed and weeded continuously, and poor or damaged materials are removed, repaired, or replaced as necessary.

Development Plan

The goal is to maintain a broadly representative collection of children's books in the CD audio format. Nonfiction spoken word titles are selected in a broad range of areas to provide access for patrons who prefer to listen rather than read. Popular materials in the junior high, fiction, and easy fiction areas are the primary emphasis of this collection. The spoken word collection will continue to have moderate growth as more children's titles become available.

	Past Collection Development Level	Current Collection Selection Level	Future Collection Development Level
Spoken Word	2	2	2

Subject: Audiovisual Sets

Description

This collection is geared toward children from six months through age four. The majority are spoken word, but some are music or instructional. The collection includes beginning-to-read materials, song and activity tapes for toddlers, language instruction, folktales, and a select collection of unabridged books on CD. Audiovisual sets for the preschooler–second grader are made up of a CD and an accompanying book. These sets are circulated as a single unit.

Influencing Factors

The collection is most heavily used by beginning readers, parents of toddlers, patrons for whom English is a second language, and reluctant readers.

Selection Plan

Selection is done primarily from publishers catalogs. Often sets are ordered through one of the journals that reviews audiovisual materials such as *School Library Journal* or *Booklist*.

Retention and Weeding

Weeding thus far has been of damaged and worn materials. Low-circulation materials should be removed.

Development Plan

The collection should be maintained by adding new release titles as they become available. Replacement copies of high-circulation titles should be purchased.

	Past Collection Development Level	Current Collection Selection Level	Future Collection Development Level
Audiovisual Sets	2-	2	2

Subject: Puppets and Books

Description

This collection consists of a book and a puppet or two of characters in that book. The books are picture books or easy nonfiction books. This collection is geared toward preschool children through second graders. The puppet and book are housed together in a blue mesh bag. These are circulated as a single unit, with the name of the puppet as the item's main entry in the library catalog.

Influencing Factors

The collection is most heavily used by parents and teachers of preschool children who use the puppets to enhance the stories they read to their children. It is a popular collection.

Selection Plan

Selection is done primarily from Folkmanis for the puppets. The books are ordered mainly from Baker and Taylor.

Retention and Weeding

Weeding thus far has been of damaged and worn materials. Low-circulation materials should be removed.

Development Plan

The collection should be maintained by adding new release titles as they become available. Replacement copies of high-circulation titles should be purchased.

	Past Collection Development Level	Current Collection Selection Level	Future Collection Development Level
Puppets and Books	2-	2	2

Subject: Big Books

Description

Big books are oversized editions of picture books and easy nonfiction books. They are housed in a custom rack that allows them to lie flat.

Influencing Factors

This collection is popular with preschool parents and teachers who can show the pictures in a big book to a group of children so that all can see them clearly.

Selection Plan

Big books are ordered mainly from Baker and Taylor and Regent. Selection is made by focusing on popular book titles and those that fit into common preschool themes.

Retention and Weeding

Weeding thus far has been of damaged and worn materials. Low-circulation materials should be removed.

Development Plan

The collection should be maintained by adding new release titles as they become available. Replacement copies of high-circulation titles should be purchased.

	Past Collection Development Level	Current Collection Selection Level	Future Collection Development Level
Big Books	2-	2	2

Subject: CD-ROMs

Description
The CD-ROM collection includes educational, informational, and "edutainment" CD-ROM programs for children from preschool through eighth grade. Programs cover the gamut of educational disciplines.

Influencing Factors
Changing technology in the CD-ROM and computer industries is a determining factor. Other influencing factors include the educational endeavors of the local schools, the needs of preschoolers and parents for early education programs, and the special needs of patrons from diverse ethnic backgrounds. Patron suggestions are encouraged.

Selection Plan
Besides the standard selection tools, publisher and vendor catalogs are used to identify available titles.

Retention and Weeding
Only those CD-ROMs with little or no circulation will be considered for weeding. CD-ROMs in poor or damaged condition will be evaluated and either removed from circulation, repaired, or replaced as necessary.

Development Plan
Curriculum needs will be weighed carefully. Patron suggestions will also be considered. Close attention must be paid to changing technologies affecting this format.

	Past Collection Development Level	Current Collection Selection Level	Future Collection Development Level
CD-ROMs	0	2	1
Preschool CD-ROMs	0	2	1

Subject: DVDs

Description

The Youth Services DVD collection consists of fiction and nonfiction films. A small number of the nonfiction films contain parent and teacher–related information and are shelved with the parent/teacher collection. Nonfiction films are shelved with nonfiction books. All films are G or PG rated.

Influencing Factors

The library acquires and makes available DVDs to serve the general informational, educational, and recreational needs of the community. Patron requests for specific DVDs will be considered and purchased if the film is appropriate to the collection for the long term. Changing technology is a factor to be considered in the long-range development of the collection.

Selection Plan

Standard selection tools and online resources are reviewed regularly. DVD selection guides located in the reference and parent/teacher collections are also used. Publishers' catalogs, distributor's catalogs (Baker and Taylor, Video Library Company, etc.), and ads are also used to identify current high-interest releases, nonfiction films, and replacements. Multiple copies are ordered for high-interest films.

Retention and Weeding

DVDs with little or no circulation, damaged items, and multiple copies are considered for weeding.

Development Plan

The DVD collection is very popular and will continue to grow in size.

	Past Collection Development Level	Current Collection Selection Level	Future Collection Development Level
DVDs	2	2	3

Description

The Come On In special needs collection includes several types of disability-related books including hi-low books and audiobooks, Boardmaker-adapted picture books, and Start-to-Finish books.

Influencing Factors

This collection is used by children and young adults with disabilities and by parents and teachers of children and young adults who have special needs.

Selection Plan

The special needs collection is ordered primarily through Usborne, Don Johnston, Academic Therapy/High Noon, and Saddleback. Leap into Literacy is the source for our adapted picture books. Our selection goal is to provide a variety of reading levels and formats that are available to children of diverse abilities.

Retention and Weeding

Books are kept as long as they continue to circulate and are in good condition. Withdrawn books may be replaced with a new copy or with a different title, in order the keep the collection fresh. The collection is analyzed and weeded each year.

Development Plan

In the near future, additional titles from currently owned series will be purchased to expand the collection. Skokie school teachers who use the collection with their students will continue to be consulted for feedback about the collection. Continuing emphasis will be on developing a well-balanced collection that will meet the diverse needs of our community's special education students.

	Past Collection Development Level	Current Collection Selection Level	Future Collection Development Level
Come On In	0	1	2

Subject: Video Games

Description

The video games are predominately entertainment oriented and are meant for children up to age 14. Games of current interest will be purchased and must have a rating of E for Everyone or Everyone 10+. Platforms will be added or dropped on the basis of popularity.

Influencing Factors

Since children see games in a variety of media, popular movies tie-ins, TV show tie-ins, book tie-ins, and sports themes will all be considered for purchase.

Selection Plan

Websites such as GameSpot and retailers that sell games can be used to identify and evaluate popular games.

Retention and Weeding

Games will be kept as long as they are still in good condition and are up-to-date enough to be played on current platforms. Games will not be withdrawn as soon as a platform is upgraded, but will be retained as long as they are being played.

Development Plan

This will be a growing collection, but no attempt will be made to buy to demand. The collection size is limited by the amount of space for storage and the high security that is needed to protect them.

	Past Collection Development Level	Current Collection Selection Level	Future Collection Development Level
Video Games	0	1+	2

IV. REVISION OF THE COLLECTION DEVELOPMENT PLAN

This collection development plan is a tool to help the library develop its collection in a systematic fashion. It must be responsive to changes in the community, in the library's mission and roles, and in the fields of book publishing and technology. The plan will be reviewed periodically in conjunction with the library's long-range planning cycle. The coordinator of Collection Development will assess the document and recommend changes to the director.

T. Room
9/08